OFF THE RAILS

OFF THE RAILS

BRITAIN'S GREAT RAIL CRISIS – CAUSE, CONSEQUENCES AND CURE

◆

ANDREW MURRAY

VERSO
London • New York

First published by Verso 2001
© Andrew Murray 2001
Foreword © John Hendy 2001
All rights reserved

2 4 6 8 10 9 7 5 3

Verso
UK: 6 Meard Street, London W1F 0EG
US: 180 Varick Street, New York, NY 10014–4606
www.versobooks.com

Verso is the imprint of New Left Books

ISBN 1-85984-640-8

British Library Cataloguing in Publication Data
A catalogue record for this book is available from the British Library

Library of Congress Cataloging-in-Publication Data
A catalog record for this book is available from the Library of Congress

Typeset by SetSystems, Saffron Walden, Essex
Printed by Biddles Ltd, Guildford and King's Lynn
www.biddles.co.uk

For Laura Murray

Contents

Foreword

I had the great honour to act as leading counsel for the bereaved and injured in the Public Inquiries into the Southall and Ladbroke Grove train crashes. Those Inquiries investigated, in the greatest detail, the events which led to those tragedies. Their wide terms of reference permitted the two Chairpersons, Professor John Uff QC and Lord Cullen, to consider recommendations to avoid recurrence in the future. But there was one area which, by their terms of reference, the Inquiries were not permitted to investigate: privatisation.

This excellent book by Andrew Murray fills the gap. He has investigated the role played by privatisation in these disasters and the subsequent one at Hatfield. His exposition leads inexorably to his conclusion that the current crisis in the rail industry can only be reversed by taking the railways back into public ownership. In my view his analysis cannot be faulted. The evidence heard in the Public Inquiries, in my personal opinion (and it can only be a personal opinion – I do not speak as an advocate here)[1] supports his conclusion.

A return of the railways to public ownership was the view of many (though not all) of the bereaved and injured, as they made clear on public platforms and in media interviews. At press conferences they expressed anger at finding that Railtrack, which receives some £1,000 million annually in public subsidy (without counting the massive supplementary payments for the consequences of Hatfield), has been distributing £350 million annually to shareholders by way of dividend from 'profits'. Not surprisingly, they considered that this money should be spent on safety.

The railways, as Andrew Murray makes clear, are in a very different position to most commercial organisations. Railtrack told the Ladbroke Grove Inquiry that it was no longer a realistic expectation that Railtrack could exist without public subsidy in the foreseeable future. Railtrack's budget is essentially controlled by a public official, the rail regulator. Railtrack is not a competitor in a free market:[2] it is a monopoly established by the state which requires a public official to prevent it abusing its position and public subsidy to survive. Consequently Railtrack barely resembles a private corporation.

There is no doubt that railway companies, in carrying out the core activities of maintaining, improving and operating the railway network and railway trains upon it, are performing a public service. The bereaved and injured also drew attention to the priority that company directors must, by law, give to the interests of the company (and hence their shareholders), which they considered to be inconsistent with the absolute precedence which should be given to the safety of passengers and staff and the public interest in general. Many concluded that the evidence they heard at the Ladbroke Grove and Southall Inquiries and the events at Hatfield showed that the privatised industry naturally inclined to inertia when faced with heavy investment in safety with little expectation of return on it. Many made clear their belief that privatisation had resulted in profit being put before safety.

A return to public ownership should reverse this tendency. But it has to be said that the nationalised industry in the years leading up to 1994 also failed to make timely safety investment, not through lack of commitment by management but precisely because it was nationalised: government controlled the budget and it deliberately starved the railway of funds. It was, for example, a government decision to abandon nationwide Automatic Train Protection (ATP) fitment. If there is to be a return to public ownership, as Andrew Murray discusses, some form of arm's length separation will be necessary. As I write, Railtrack shares are valued at only 58p each. It might be thought that now would be an opportune time for the new government to buy them.

The history of safety on the railways in private hands is both long and uninspiring. Just as in recent times the privatised industry failed to motivate itself to introduce Train Protection and Warning System (TPWS) until Parliament introduced legislation (in 1999) which required it to do so, and just as the industry admitted in the Joint Inquiry that it needed the spur of further regulations (to be introduced in the next year or two) to compel it to fit European Train Control System (ETCS), so in the past there has been a consistent and shameful need for legislation to compel the introduction of obvious safety measures which the industry failed to fit by reason of cost. Thus for example,[3] a Bill was introduced in Parliament in 1876 requiring that 'every train should be povided with sufficient brake power to stop it absolutely within 500 yards at the highest speed at which it travels and upon any gradient.'

The Bill was defeated by the combined influence of the 120 railway directors in Parliament. An insight into their attitude may be gleaned from the comments of the General Manager of the London, Dover & Chatham Railway to his shareholders in relation to continuous brakes and other safety measures. He was reported as saying that he 'had had these things urged upon him for some time but he had been reluctant to involve the shareholders in a single shilling of outlay which could be avoided.' He required 'not mere theory but the strongest evidence that these things were required.'

In the event it took the terrible Armagh disaster of June 12 1889[4] to create the pressure to cause the passage of the Regulation of Railways Act 1889 which imposed the requirement of the use of continuous fail-safe braking.

The parallels between this historical vignette and the events recounted by Andrew Murray are only too obvious.

The history of ATP and its European equivalent, ETCS, may be thought to show the same symptoms. Professor Uff, in his report on the Southall crash, highlighted 'lack of commitment' and 'outright hostility' to the installation of ATP. His conclusion was that 'all the foregoing problems and their resolution could have occurred within a very much shorter time span had there been greater commitment and allocation of resources in the period before and following privatisation.'

It took twelve years before ATP was fully operational on Great Western Trains (GWT) and the Chiltern line. Since the Ladbroke Grove disaster, GWT have operated a policy of 'no ATP, no run'. Thames Trains (whose Turbo train was crushed at Ladbroke Grove) had rejected fitting ATP on the basis of a cost-benefit analysis in 1996 which was heavily criticised by the bereaved and injured (and defended by Thames Trains) at the Inquiry. Without the disasters of Southall and Ladbroke Grove, the suspicion of the bereaved and injured was that ATP might have been abandoned altogether on Britain's railways.

In 1988 the Hidden Report into the Clapham rail disaster stated:

B[ritish] R[ailways] B[oard] is responsible for an industry where concern for safety should be at the forefront of the minds of everyone, from the Board itself at the top to the newest beginner at the bottom. The concept of absolute safety must be a gospel spread across the whole workforce and paramount in the minds of management.[5]

Why was it not? Why did the railway industry fail to grasp the danger posed by the Paddington layout, perhaps the primary cause of the Ladbroke Grove crash,[6] by the scruff of the neck? Why were regulations and the force of law required to compel the installation of TPWS and ETCS? Why were the rails not renewed at Hatfield? Andrew Murray answers these questions by reference to privatisation. In this he has some support from the HSE.

Ms Bacon, then Director of the Health and Safety Executive said:

. . . what also comes across is the gradual reduction of trust in the industry after privatisation. The idea of BR's public sector responsibility as something to be relied on has died hard, and indeed was perpetuated by Railtrack's initial assertion that it was the 'directing mind' for safety on the railway. Reality has not lived up to expectation . . .

Thus the 'HSE detected growing reluctance by BR – and still more by the newly established Railtrack . . . to introduce ATP at all.'

According to the HSE Director, Railtrack's position was 'to do the minimum that the Government would accept'.

She added:

> The present regulatory approach does not appear to offer sufficient assurance to the public because the commercialised rail industry is also subject to pressures from the economic regulator and from shareholders . . . To compensate for this, there is an expectation of far greater regulatory involvement. Certainly the Executive now thinks that more intervention than was originally envisaged is both justified and necessary in the light of experience of how the industry in fact operates.

Privatisation of Britain's railways has also created other problems, as Andrew Murray makes clear. One such is the inevitable fragmentation created not only by divorcing the track from the trains but also because in private industry there is an economic imperative in 'outsource' and subcontract. The result has been to create some 120 major commerical parties in the industry with hundreds more minor subcontractors. Some have estimated that there are some 2,000 companies now involved. As Professor Uff pointed out in his Report into Southall:

> The difficulties resulting from fragmentation can be divided into two categories: first, those resulting from overlapping functions and lack of clear boundaries; secondly, those resulting from artificially divided responsibilities.

As significant, in my view, has been that these entities are now in competition rather than co-operation. Their relationships are no longer dominated by loyalty to a common purpose of public service under a central command but by a myriad of contracts. Hundreds of lawyer hours on each side are devoted to trying to create a legal document which will extract the maximum benefit for the respective client. This is not necessarily incompatible with the benefit of the third parties, such as the passengers, but the achievement of that benefit may be a matter of chance.

A single organisation, the railway cannot be satisfactorily run exclusively by legal contractual relations. Tightly specified contracts are incapable of creating co-operative commitment to safety: no contract can ever eliminate the space for parties not to pursue its terms wholeheartedly. Management by contractual relationship seems particularly inappropriate where an enterprise is required to put long-term issues of public interest ahead of its own immediate short-term interests. Cracks must inevitably exist between the components of the fragmented rail industry. Through these safety may slip. The fragility of papering over them with contracts is apparent.

Andrew Murray's book is a masterful analysis of the role of privatisation in the crisis currently facing Britain's railways. How differently they do things abroad. As I write, the French railways, SNCF, have announced the opening of the TGV from Paris to Marseilles, cutting journey times to two and a half hours. It is anticipated that this will have a major benefit for the French economy. Andrew Murray shows a way in which we may re-join the leaders of this globalised world in which communication and transport systems play a key part.

John Hendy QC
London, June 2001

The existing culture [within BR] is more about keeping the trains running than market-oriented thrust – John MacGregor, Secretary of State for Transport, 1993

We had perfectly decent standards for wheels, perfectly decent standards for rail, but where the two touch perhaps hasn't had the attention it might have done. – Railtrack spokesman, 2001

They destroyed a railway that took more than 150 years to develop, and I for one shall never forgive them. – Peter Rayner, former director of British Rail, 2001

Introduction and Acknowledgements

It didn't even seem like a good idea at the time. The privatisation of Britain's railways was flawed in principle and even more so in practice. It deserves a special place in the annals of entirely man-made disasters.

Britain was the birthplace of the railway. The first rail network in the world survived 150 years of peace and war, from Victorian buccaneering enterprise to optimistic nationalisation. It has taken little more than five years of a bizarre, fragmented privatisation under a regime of blundering mismanagement to bring it to its knees.

It comes to this: in January 2001, a spokesman for Railtrack admitted that while they had got the track right, and the train wheels right, they had not yet been able to get the relationship of the two, 'where they touch', right. It's a long way from Isambard Kingdom Brunel and George Stephenson.

•   •   •

This is the story of what has happened to our trains and why. How 'market thrust' led to immobility. How 'competition' ended in catastrophe. It is a story which twenty years ago would have been dismissed as wild fiction, and which twenty years hence will find a place in those management seminars which teach by negative example.

There is no shortage of explanations as to what went wrong. The then Chief Executive of Railtrack, Gerald Corbett, set a heroic example in this respect at least in the weeks between the terrible crash at Hatfield in October 2000 and his own enforced resignation. He blamed everything on the wrong sort of trains. On the wrong sort of structure of the industry. On the wrong sort of regulators.

On all these points, he has something of an argument. This book makes a different case, however. Privatisation, motivated by political malice and lubricated by greed, is responsible for the collapse of our railways. It is the politicians of the last government, the ones who engineered this disaster, who deserve to be in the dock. As time goes by, the case for them to be joined by those politicians in the present government who have refused to address the consequences grows stronger.

The heart of the case for the prosecution here is the testimony of those who work in the industry itself. It is in the words of train drivers, signallers, guards, maintenance workers, contracts managers and others that we can build up the most vivid picture of how fragmentation in the interests of private profit has overwhelmed a railway once run in the public interest.

That is Chapter 4. The earlier chapters seek to set the scene. Chapter 1 sketches, very briefly, the development of the railway system in Britain up to the point of privatisation, and explains what the Conservative government felt it was trying to do, and why so many people told them they were daft. It includes a brief defence of the project which John Major was kind enough to supply. A letter soliciting an interview with John MacGregor, his Transport Secretary at the critical stages of privatisation, went unanswered.

Chapter 2 explains the almost unbelievable structure of the privatised railway created by the Conservatives, and looks at who has benefited from it and how. It also examines the record of the privatised industry in terms of efficiency and investment.

The most serious indictment of privatisation is, of course, in respect of safety. Chapter 3 addresses this. The accidents at Southall, Ladbroke Grove and Hatfield are examined, and their rather different immediate causes traced back to a common root in privatisation.

Following on from the front-line dispatches mentioned above – the voices of the railway employees themselves – Chapter 5 deals with the great rail crisis of 2000–2001, when the post-Hatfield paralysis finally forced the country and politicians alike to confront what had been done to the railway, and the impossibility of the industry as it was constituted under privatisation ever to set things right again.

Finally, Chapter 6 considers the alternatives to the present mayhem. It examines the palliative reforms proposed by government, but the bulk of it is devoted to what I hope is the clear and compelling case for a return of the railways to public ownership.

•　　　•　　　•

Although this book is essentially about the British railways, I hope that it also serves to focus attention on a larger issue: the political and economic legacy of the 1980s, in respect of privatisation in particular. Privatisation has developed from a fringe notion cooked up in right-wing think tanks into an almost unalterable dogma applied to just about everything throughout the world. The experience of rail privatisation in Britain, while perhaps uniquely awful, has a wider message. It is time for this particular dogma to be re-examined in public debate. If this book helps that happen, its purpose will have been well served.

Acknowledgements

I would like to thank those friends and colleagues who have been kind enough to assist, in one way or another, in the writing of this book – Bruce Allan, Jane Barker, Nick Cole, Rob Griffiths, Joy Johnson, Anna Kruthoffer, Seumas Milne, Dave Nixon, Frances O'Grady, Mick Rix, Martin Samways, Jennifer Smith and Jennie Walsh. None of them, of course, bear any responsibility for either errors or the author's opinions.

Thanks as well to Colin Robinson and his colleagues at Verso who have been most supportive throughout. Many thanks also to John Hendy for kindly agreeing to write the very informative Foreword.

Particular thanks must go to those who can only be acknowledged anonymously – the many employees of the railway industry who agreed to be interviewed and gave me invaluable additional insights and assistance. Roll on the day when they can speak openly about the industry for which they care so deeply.

Andrew Murray
London, May 2001

Glossary of Abbreviations

ASLEF	Associated Society of Locomotive Engineers and Firemen (train drivers' union)
ATP	Automatic Train Protection
AWS	Automatic Warning System
BR	British Rail
DETR	Department of Environment, Transport and the Regions
ETCS	European Train Control System
FOC	freight operating company
GNER	Great North Eastern Railway
GWR	Great Western Railway
HMRI	Her Majesty's Railway Inspectorate (part of the HSE)
HSE	Health and Safety Executive
INFRACO	infrastructure maintenance company

NEG	National Express Group
ORR	Office of the Rail Regulator
RMT	Rail Maritime and Transport Union
ROSCO	rolling stock leasing company
SPAD	signal passed at danger
SRA	Strategic Rail Authority
TOC	train operating company
TPWS	Train Protection and Warning System
TRUST	Train Running System (used for monitoring and attributing causes of delays on the network)
TSSA	Transport Salaried Staffs Association
WAGN	West Anglia Great Northern railway

1

Trains and Money

After any tragedy there is a hunt to find someone to blame. At least in the tragi-comedy of the privatisation of Britain's railways, we have not had to look very far. The buck stops with Conservative ministers mesmerised by a vision.

Take Roger Freeman. He deserves to be remembered as one of the Tory Ministry of Transport team of the early 1990s which turned privatisation of the railways into practical reality. His vision came to him in the course of a family holiday spent on Russia's famous Trans-Siberian Railway. The service was slow and unreliable, he told a reporter on his return. 'The Trans-Siberian route will be impossible within five years,' he said. 'I do not want to see that on British Rail.'[1]

'Beware the voices', it is tempting to say. In 2001, the Trans-Siberian is still rolling along, while Mr Freeman's vision has, within five years of its implementation, brought the old BR network to a grinding halt. Were Russia's railways to mount a takeover bid, Britain's passengers would probably hail them as saviours.

How did we get here? Railway privatisation is the latest stop along a line where all the main halts for the last hundred years have been marked 'rundown', 'no investment' and 'cutback'. The privatis-ation of British Rail, however, has proved to be not merely a crisis for the railways, but also a crisis for the whole cherished privatisation project, the private = good, public = bad equation, which has trans-formed much of the economic landscape in Britain and around the world over the last generation.

Perhaps it is fitting that the prime example of the whole privatisa-tion epoch of the 1980s and 1990s should have been that of the railways, for the development of rail and the development of capital-ism in Britain have marched hand in hand since the earliest days.

Pioneers of capitalism

The initial development of the railways marked a quantum leap in the organisation of capital. Requiring a far higher level of investment, with returns spread over a longer period, than the textile mills previously typical of early industrial capitalism, the railways virtually gave birth to the joint-stock company. Unlike mine and mill, the construction of a railway required the mobilisation of the money of many people.

The railways were the sinews of the new economy, enabling local industry to move beyond a national market, and the distributers of industrial staples like coal or cotton to move beyond the limitations of canal transport. Rail also helped develop the national capital market, with small shareholders in the railway companies becoming the first generation of 'Sids', as small investors in the British Gas privatisation promotion more than a century later became known. Over 40 per cent of the shares in the South-East Railway, for example, were held by investors living in Lancashire or Cheshire.

The largest of the Victorian railway companies – the London &
North-Western, or the Midland – ranked among the largest companies of any type, anywhere in the world. A world away from
today's franchised train operators who own little more than their
brand, these companies were vertically integrated concerns, in some
cases manufacturing their own rolling stock, as well as owning the
track, running the trains and stations and carrying out their own
maintenance and repairs. At its pinnacle, it is estimated that railway
investment in Britain amounted to 45 per cent of the national total.[2]

Indeed, by 1881, capital invested in the railways was equal to the
national debt of the UK, and by the end of the nineteenth century
amounted to over one billion pounds, an extraordinary sum for the
time.[3]

As with other British industries, the railway companies rode the
wave of imperialism, exporting capital, machinery and skilled engineers to all points of the globe, making the railways pioneers not
merely of British money but of the British Empire and its traditions
as well.

At the same time, there began to emerge the first signs of a
tendency to neglect the levels of investment necessary to properly
maintain an already extensive network of domestic railways, while at
the same time keeping the shareholders happy. Railway investment
ebbed and flowed with the overall trade cycle of Victorian England,
and profitability generally started to decline. The high level of costs
sunk in infrastructure construction meant that servicing debt became
increasingly difficult during economic downturns. The turn of the
century saw the last major wave of new line building in Britain,
including the Great Central route from the midlands to London's
Marylebone station, as the network reached virtual saturation point.

War and grouping

From that point on, the financial position of the great railway companies tended to deteriorate. Diminishing rates of return on capital led to a falling off in investment. Given the essential economic and strategic role of the railways at that time, this could not but bring the industry into an ever-closer embrace by the state. Government could not allow the system to collapse, free-market dogma notwithstanding.

New Labour ministers, equally convinced of the efficacy of private enterprise, are now rediscovering this unavoidable reality in our own times. Despite many real and apparent changes in the management of the railways since, the relationship of government to the industry remained intimate from the Great War onwards.

The 1914–18 conflict imposed great demands on the railway network, caught up as it was in the first great mobilisation of the nation-state in the twentieth century. 50 per cent of railway staff of military age and 600 locomotives were mobilised for the Empire's war effort. At the same time, the conflict meant that resources for investment were increasingly directed elsewhere, particularly towards the new manufacturing and chemical industries which the conflict required.

The government took control of the railways during the war, establishing a Railway Executive Committee, on which were represented the general managers (chief executives of their day) of the largest companies. This form of quasi-nationalisation was ended in 1921, when the railways were returned to private control, with a £60 million dowry from the Treasury as compensation for the years of state supervision.

However, they were not returned to their pre-war state. The 120 railway companies of the Edwardian era, some of which did compete with each other, were rationalised by government fiat into four groups – Southern, London Midland Scottish, London North-Eastern and Great Western – a structure carried through to the British Rail regions of the nationalised era. This measure of consolidation failed, nevertheless, to lead to a revival of the railways. It was, however, a recognition by Conservative politicians that the free market and competition were not on their own sufficient guarantors of a success-ful railway industry.

Although the railways retained a virtual monopoly of the long-distance (and much short-distance) movement of goods and people, they could not escape the consequences of the general slump in trade and economic activity which characterised the first years after the war, and the whole period from 1929 onwards. The start of serious competition from motor vehicles added to the pressure. Investment slipped below the levels required to maintain the overall network even in its prevailing state, with the result that by 1939, despite some government support, the railways wore an increasingly dilapidated air in many parts.

The rate of return on capital fell to just 2.9 per cent, not enough to excite the appetites of many investors. The Southern Railway, for example, offered its shareholders a dividend of only 0.65 per cent, while the LNER offered nothing at all in the years immediately before World War II!

It was scarcely surprising, then, that the proposal for nationalisa-tion advanced by the Attlee government after its 1945 election victory did not arouse the opposition which might have been expected. Nationalisation had, in fact, been around as an idea since the turn of the century, with many liberals and nationalists joining socialists amongst its advocates, arguing the case on grounds of national efficiency and planning as much as public service or social equality. World War II strengthened this argument. The indispensable role of the railways in moving both capital and people around the country at a time of mass bombing had underlined their role as a key part of the war effort.

Nationalisation

On December 31 1947, the railways became the property of the state. Again, the fate of the industry mirrored the tenor of the times. Railway nationalisation formed part of a sweeping programme of state ownership carried through by the Labour government elected in 1945.

Like the other nationalisation initiatives of the time, this also had a dual character. It was defensive in so far as it represented the state stepping in to take over an essential service which was deteriorating unacceptably under private ownership, and it was also forward looking in so far as it helped lay the basis for a more sweeping reorganisation of transport and industry as a whole on a planned basis. In practice it was the former aspect – managing decline – which predominated throughout the history of the nationalised railway.

Shareholders in the big four companies received compensation through government bonds representing a claim on the newly created British Transport Commission (BTC). Returns were guaranteed at 3 per cent, a very good deal bearing in mind the pre-war rate of return. This arrangement worked more to the benefit of the shareholder than the public, since it helped perpetuate the industry's problem of generating sufficient funds for investment purposes.

Nationalisation did not, however, fulfil the hopes which other sections of the community had vested in it to anything like the same extent as the generously compensated shareholders. The inadequacies of control by the stock market and private enterprise were replaced by a stringent Treasury regime which appeared to begrudge every penny spent on improving the network. Indeed, since many of the old private railway directors were put in charge of the new nationalised industry, the railways could be said to have had the worst of both worlds.

Given that the nationalised years were also the years which saw road transport finally emerge as a full-blooded competitor to the railways, this was a crippling disadvantage, even though road haulage was also initially under the auspices of the state-owned BTC. The same governments which stinted nothing in girdling the country with motorways from the end of the 1950s onwards passed up almost every chance to modernise the railways in order to meet the new competition. A politically powerful 'road lobby' emerged to ensure that this remained the case. Under these circumstances, the image of the railways as an industry locked in irreversible decline became a self-fulfilling prophecy.

Gradually, the railways were switched from steam to diesel or electric traction, although government was still haggling about electrifying major lines more than twenty years after this became technically feasible (by which point the proportion of the network electrified was the lowest in Europe). A modernisation plan agreed in 1955 was only half implemented before the arrival of the notorious Dr Beeching as British Rail chairman.

Driven by the obsessive insistence of governments of both parties that the railways should aim to break even financially and thereby avoid becoming a charge on the Exchequer, a culture of closures – now sweeping, as under Beeching, now piecemeal – took hold. Rail's share of freight traffic fell from around 50 per cent in the 1950s to less than 10 per cent just twenty years later, while passengers increasingly took to publicly-subsidised roads, which no one expected to become self-sustaining profit centres.

However, British Rail was far from either a commercial or public service disaster. Its safety record was generally excellent, and its service reliability, when not disrupted by the industrial relations problems common throughout British industry in those years, much better than the conventional wisdom of the day would have it. By the late 1980s, moreover, two of BR's four main divisions – Inter-City and Railfreight – were profitable, although the other two – provincial services and the south-east commuter network – still required prodigious subventions from the taxpayer, as they do today.

At the time privatisation began to be mooted, fully 71 per cent of British Rail's costs were covered by fares, a figure only matched throughout Europe by Sweden's railways. Even Tory ministers acknowledged the productivity of the workforce. The price, however, was paid in the investment needed to maintain and develop a modern railway system. British Rail invested just 26.4 pence per train kilometre per year, a sum equivalent to 8.9 per cent of costs. The comparable figures for France were 70.3 pence (15.6 per cent of costs), for West Germany £1.284 (26.1 per cent of costs) and for Austria £2.154, or 38.8 per cent of costs. Those seeking a reason for the dilapidated state of Britain's railways compared to those in continental Europe need look no further than these figures.[4]

The Tories

Margaret Thatcher's rise to power complicated the position of the railways still further. Her government disliked state-run industries on principle, and she herself disliked trains in particular, travelling on the railways just once throughout the eleven years of her premiership. In her first years in office, her government accordingly helped make the unprofitability of British Rail chronic by forcing the corporation to divest itself of its money-making subsidiaries in areas like hotels and shipping. The government also commissioned the notorious Serpell report, giving it a brief to find ways of cutting the railway's losses. Serpell's suggestions of sweeping cutbacks were so extreme, however, that ministers could not pursue them, but neglect through cash squeezes was maintained. Under Thatcher, the real cost of car travel dropped, while that of public transport, both on road and rail, rose rapidly.

Nevertheless, Mrs Thatcher herself remained sceptical about the possibility of privatising British Rail, displaying a political sensitivity which in this case over-rode her missionary zeal for unfettered capitalism. There were, of course, plenty of privatisation opportunities elsewhere in the 1980s and gradually the Conservatives worked their way through the state sector of the economy, turning aerospace, airlines, telephones, gas, electricity, coal and finally water over to private business.

It would be a digression to consider the subject in detail here, but it should be noted that privatisation did contribute considerably to the buoyancy of the public finances throughout the Thatcher years. The funds raised from sell-offs became a sort of narcotic for the

Treasury, driving mandarins into a frenzied search for the next financial fix from a further privatisation, however improbable.

In addition, privatisation created a chimera of 'popular capitalism', with millions of small shareholders coming to the market for the first time. This would dissipate in time, as, amongst other developments, shareholdings in the privatised industries re-consolidated rapidly in the hands of the big financial institutions. But these institutions themselves were given a massive shot in the arm by privatisation, and a whole class of speculators, advisers, merchant bankers, legal experts, financiers, mergers and acquisitions specialists and all the rest grew fat on the proceeds of the great privatisations. They came to expect continued large dividends from post-privatisation asset stripping.

The mandarins and the merchant bankers were therefore not going to leave the railways alone indefinitely, despite Mrs Thatcher's scepticism. All that was required was a final dash of hubris, which was supplied by John Major's unexpected victory at the 1992 general election, a triumph which led many Tories to believe that their hold on power was unshakeable, and to behave accordingly. The brief humiliation of the Poll Tax was forgotten, and the scene was set for what Simon Jenkins of *The Times* was to call the 'Poll Tax on wheels'.

Planning privatisation

Selling off the railways was an idea first hatched in the hard right circles of the Conservative think-tanks. The two best known, the

Centre for Policy Studies (CPS) and the Adam Smith Institute, each came up with their own scheme in the mid-1980s. The Adam Smith Institute advocated a version of the plan that eventually became accepted – with the separation of infrastructure ownership from train operation at its core.

The CPS had argued for a return to vertically integrated private companies, owning track and train alike, seeking to create as far as possible a railway map similar to that prior to the 1921 amalgamations. What is now of interest in the CPS position, however, is the critique it made of the rival Adam Smith Institute plan.

Creating a Railtrack monopoly, the CPS argued, would generate no incentive towards efficiency, would likely show a tendency to let assets deteriorate and would be over-complex. 'The separation of track and train would mean that there would be no unitary point in the management structure.'[5] Prescient words, but they were not heeded.

The third privatisation option, 'BR plc' – the sell-off of British Rail intact on the market – was never given serious consideration, despite the fact that this option had been the means of privatisation most commonly adopted by the government hitherto. When he eventually came to announce privatisation to the House of Commons, Transport Secretary John MacGregor explained his decision thus: 'British Rail is dependent on substantial subsidy from government and makes large losses. So it is not possible to sell all of BR either as a single entity, or as separate businesses.'

Here he put his finger, unwittingly, on the central dilemma and the ultimate tragedy of railway privatisation in Britain: how to turn a subsidised public service into an attractive collection of profit centres? It was by following the logic of this question to the end that

MacGregor, Major and their colleagues ended up with a plan to split British Rail into around 100 different pieces, and sell each of them to somebody different.

One other factor must also be taken into the reckoning. Barely had the Conservatives got over the shock of their re-election in June 1992 than events in the autumn (the forced exit of Britain from the European exchange rate mechanism after the defence of a policy that cost upwards of a million jobs, followed by a huge political storm over the pit-closure programme) made it pretty clear that ministers did not have life tenure on their portfolios after all. The earlier Thatcherite hubris dissolved into a panicky desire to complete that last great privatisation while it was still politically possible.

The horizon for a complex privatisation was thus dramatically telescoped. It had to be done – and preferably made irreversible – within four and a half years at the most. So haste was added to the combustible cocktail of ideological intransigence and greed. Indeed, one authoritative account of the railway privatisation has even suggested that such was MacGregor's haste that he did not even have time to properly study the options, or the detail of the model he was proposing. His deputy Roger Freeman has conceded that there was 'no time' for a full debate.[6]

Certainly, the scheme for privatisation finally laid before parliament in 1992 was extraordinary. Its broad outlines are by now familiar. A track authority was to be established which was to own the entire infrastructure – tracks, signalling, stations, other railway land. This was to be Railtrack, which was slated for sell-off at a later date.

The train services to be run over this infrastructure were to be operated by twenty-five different franchises, ranging from large long-

distance operations hewn from the old Inter-City routes to complicated suburban networks around London down to small regionally
based businesses. These franchises were to be let for varying terms to
private firms, the winner of each franchise being the one who would
offer to run it with the lowest subsidy from the taxpayer within the
broad service guidelines laid down.

The trains themselves would not be owned by these enterprises
but by three specially created leasing companies, called ROSCOs,
which were themselves to be privatised. BR's rolling stock was to be
handed over to these firms, which would in turn lease them to the
franchisees on seven-year contracts with terms dictated by government in favour of the ROSCOs in order to justify the price of their
sales.

Nor would the infrastructure be maintained by its owner, Railtrack. Instead, British Rail's maintenance and repair services were
themselves divided into thirteen, and sold to the highest bidder.
Many of these firms would themselves, of course, subcontract out
much of their labour-intensive work, as is the way in construction-
related industries.

Train repair and heavy maintenance works were themselves sold
off separately, as were a host of smaller BR enterprises operating in
fields from consultancy to communications.

Interestingly, the final scheme bore some resemblance to proposals
first advanced by senior managers of the privatised railway when
trying to stave off full nationalisation after the war. Michael Bonavia,
then an executive of the London and North-Eastern Railway, and
later its official historian, writes: 'I . . . drafted a paper proposing a
"mixed" transport organisation including public and private ownership. The railway boards and managements would continue but

would sell their track, signalling and structures to the State. They would then be granted a franchise to operate with their own loco-motives, rolling stock etc.'

The scheme came to nothing in 1947, and the Tories of the Thatcher–Major era were having nothing of 'mixed' ownership. Although Railtrack was initially to be retained in the public sector, this policy was soon reversed by a Treasury eager for the extra receipts and ministers keen to make their privatisation irreversible.

One misapprehension sometimes encountered is the idea that the misguided proposal adopted was forced on an unwilling British body politic by the European Union. Such a notion is far from the truth. There is little or no indication that Conservative ministers were inspired by orders from Brussels.

In fact, such orders did not exist. The relevant document is EC directive 91/440. This mandates national railway operations to keep separate accounts for infrastructure and train operation, in order to promote 'transparency' about the costs of cross-border journeys. The directive sets this in the context of market mechanisms in general, but it is silent on the question of the ownership of railways, or even as to whether they may be managed as a single enterprise.

The directive declares sweepingly that 'member states may exclude from the scope of this directive railway undertakings whose activity is limited to the provision of solely urban, suburban or regional services'. Elsewhere it allows that 'it is appropriate for member states to retain general responsibility for the development of the appropriate railway infrastructure'.[7]

No, the drive for privatisation came from British Conservative hearts alone. It is important for this to be understood, lest any politicians of any party today declare that EU rules make a return to public ownership impossible (notwithstanding Brussels' undoubted preference for private over public enterprise).

Having thus shattered the integrated railway network, with its culture of service, the government set about creating a fresh structure based primarily on intra-industry contracts, with a culture of profit maximisation and cost reduction (all on top of swingeing subsidy and staffing cuts imposed by government during the privatisation process). The different sections of the fragmented railway related to each other through contracts specifying services expected, complete with fines for failure or non-delivery. This was to be supervised by a brace of regulators, one of whom would hand out franchises, while the other would, amongst other things, approve the access charges which Railtrack could levy from the franchisees.

It was a scheme only a lawyer could love. As the *Financial Times* columnist Joe Rogaly observed at the time: 'A hundred public companies, which must draw up a mountain of contracts between them, will present our old friends in the legal profession with a fortune equivalent to the one their great-grandfathers made from the spread of the railways in the nineteenth century.'[8]

Certainly, it was a scheme which found few other advocates. Nicholas Ridley, an arch-privatising Trade Secretary in the Thatcher years, said flatly 'I do not believe it is possible to privatise the railways', while Lord Young, another die-hard Thatcherite, wondered 'if we aren't trying to privatise some things which basically can't or shouldn't be privatised'.[9]

Opposition to privatisation was spearheaded in the Commons by the chair of the Transport Committee, Robert Adley, and in the Lords by Lord Peyton, both Conservatives. Adley's committee was an unsparing critic. Its report on the government's proposals, published in April 1993, would have given pause to less self-assured, or arrogant, ministers. Among its conclusions:

— Franchises, to be effective, should include elements of 'vertical integration', allowing operators some control over track and signalling.
— Railtrack and the franchising authority, should be merged into a single public rail authority.
— British Rail should be allowed to bid for franchises against private sector bidders.
— Network benefits, such as the cross-validity of tickets, should be protected.

These suggestions, an attempt by a Conservative-dominated committee to find a meeting point between the government's proposals and the realities of running a railway, are worth noting as in some respects pointing a way out of the chaos today.[10]

As for Labour, John Prescott could not have been clearer at the party's 1993 conference: 'Any privatisation of the railway system that does take place will, on the arrival of a Labour government, be quickly and effectively dealt with, with the full support of the community, and returned to public ownership.'[11]

In 1995, in the run-up to the special Labour conference which scrapped Clause Four of the party's constitution, embodying its historic commitment to public ownership, Blair and Prescott were both nevertheless keen to emphasise that a Labour government would see the restoration of a 'publicly-owned, publicly-accountable railway'.

It was only in 1996 that Labour executed a U-turn on this issue, as it did on so many others at the time, apparently determined to fight the forthcoming general election without the trace of any policy which might offend the City of London or the financial institutions. Talk of a publicly owned railway was abandoned in favour of additional regulation.

The Liberal Democrats, for their part, took the view that 'in areas of strategic significance such as the development of our rail network ... public ownership is more appropriate than fragmented and inevitably short term private sector involvement.' Transport spokesman Paul Tyler also committed his party to work for the return of Railtrack to the public sector, should it be privatised.[12]

Criticism was as sharp from the professionals as it was from the politicians. Bill Bradshaw, a transport academic who for many years had been a senior BR manager, wrote that the proposal to establish a separate track authority contradicted all principles of railway operation and was 'likely to result in an outcome which will be unsuitable, expensive and unsafe'.[13]

According to opinion surveys, this view was representative of that of a majority of railway executives. The white-collar rail union TSSA surveyed its members in BR's executive grades and found only 7 per cent in favour of the government's plan, with 92 per cent against.[14]

Sir Bob Reid, BR's chairman at the time, expressed the heretical view that 'a railway should meet the social needs of the country as well as the economic needs ... whether the best way of doing that is by breaking up the railway I have doubts.'[15]

And one other leading industrialist expressed himself before Adley's Transport Committee as 'deeply sceptical about the proposals ... investors will be deterred by the clapped-out services; they will cherry pick the lines that have seen investment.'

The world at large was equally unimpressed. From a country where the trains do run on time, Mashai Matsuda, President of Japanese Railways East, said: 'I have looked at the way they are trying to privatise British Rail. And I know it will fail.' *Jane's World Railways*, international bible of the industry, was equally scornful.[16]

The avalanche of criticism failed to deflect Mr Major's government from its purpose, one of the few areas in which that hapless administration was not blown off course. It has been suggested that the prime minister was in part motivated by a desire to achieve something which his predecessor, still casting a long shadow over the Tory party, had not and by a wish to display Thatcherite resolution in one area at least. Certainly, his determination to proceed, in the teeth of such broad opposition, with the most unpopular privatisation ever, still requires adequate explanation.

In the course of preparing this book, I wrote to Mr Major asking him for an interview in which to explain and defend, if he wished, railway privatisation. He courteously declined by letter in March 2001, but did outline his views:

I would like to set out why I believed – and continue to believe – that privatisation was right and the only way in which we will provide a modern, efficient railway service with up to date rolling stock.

In all the years from nationalisation, British Rail was underfunded. This was not due to malice on the part of any government, but because when measured against the demands of health, education, pensions and social services, it always fell down the order of priorities.

I saw this very clearly in the decade before privatisation and believed that only by returning it to the private sector and giving it access to the capital markets would adequate long-term investment be ensured. It was essentially for this reason that I was ... pre-disposed to privatisation, and I think the scale of post-privatisation investment suggests that the resources to provide the sort of railway service you and I would both wish to see are now being provided. There is, of course, a huge backlog to make up and a long way to go, but funds would never have been provided in sufficient quantity under any Government and now I believe they will.

When we examine the investment record of the private industry, the truth is a little more complex than that, not least in so far as the great bulk of investment in railways in 2001 continues to come from the taxpayer, including nearly all money for major new projects. However, the former prime minister is undoubtedly right when he argues that British Rail had been starved of investment (although comparison with roads might be more relevant than comparison with health or education). The Thatcher government of the 1980s had been the worst offender in this regard. What he did not attempt to defend in his letter to me was the form of privatisation which he adopted nine years ago.

That form, concocted in haste, was implemented with even greater rapidity. With ministers snapping at his heels, the first franchising director managed to sell off all twenty-five franchises before the 1997 general election, lubricated with the promise of generous taxpayers' subsidies. He refused to permit bids from British Rail for any of them.

As a final act of almost pure spite, the dwindling Conservative majority rushed through the privatisation of Railtrack just in time for their rendezvous with the voters in 1997. This was despite the circumstance, unique among the privatisation projects, that Railtrack relied on increasing sums of taxpayers' money for most of its revenue (the subsidies paid to the franchise operators being passed on to Railtrack in access charges). Still worse, the structure devised for the industry guaranteed that this newly unleashed monopoly would seek that part of its fortune not underwritten by the Treasury at the expense of every other company in the privatised industry – with disastrous results.

In words which sounded an early warning of the problems which would ultimately lead to the disaster at Hatfield in October 2000, a *Daily Telegraph* article on Railtrack's sell-off observed that 'because track access charges are set by the regulator, the key to Railtrack's profitability is the reduction of costs, the majority of which are accounted for by maintenance.'[17]

Indeed, Railtrack saw its future profitability along two lines of activity – cutting the cost of maintaining the rail network, and spectacular projects in the field of property development. To help it on its way, the government wrote off £1,459 million in debt, before selling the company off for a total of £1.9 billion (a knock-down price that represented less than a third of the company's asset value), thereby dismantling and disposing of the final publicly owned piece of British Rail. The entire cost to the taxpayer of the whole privatisation exercise – from the consultants' fees through to the undervaluation of assets – has been authoritatively estimated at a little under six billion pounds.[18]

Rail privatisation was essentially an act of dogma. Who can doubt this when its principal parliamentary architect, John MacGregor, defended his plans in these words: 'The existing culture [within BR] is more about keeping the trains running than market-oriented thrust'.

For ministers drunk on their triumphs of the 1980s, a railway management content merely to 'keep the trains running' was confessing to its own inadequacy. How much travellers today must long for a return of the 'existing culture'. No one has been getting anywhere propelled by 'market-oriented thrust'.[19]

One error alone was made by critics of the scheme at the time of its first presentation. It was made by Lord Marsh, a former BR chairman, who attacked the scheme on the grounds that private operators would not be able to make any money out of it. Oh, but they have.

2

The One Hundred Piece Railway

'**O**ur objective is to improve the quality of railway services by creating many new opportunities for private sector involvement. This will mean more competition, greater efficiency and a wider choice of services more closely tailored to what customers want.'

Thus John MacGregor in his foreword to the government's 1992 white paper outlining its plans to privatise British Rail.

So much for objectives. The reality in 2001 shows four bus companies dominating train operation, one track monopoly showering its shareholders with taxpayers' cash, a few construction firms bringing the practices of the building site to railway maintenance, and three banks owning all our trains.

The key concept for Mr MacGregor was undoubtedly 'competition'. The search for a way of creating a competitive market in the railway industry had been the cornerstone of Conservative thinking on the issue since the 1980s, when the right-wing think-tanks had first turned their minds to the issue.

The search for competition on the tracks displayed an astonishing lack of understanding of either the history or even the technical limitations of the railways in Britain. Since the first world war at the latest, and to some extent even earlier, competition between railway companies for moving either people or goods had been of declining significance. In fact, wasteful competition (including the construction in some cases of nearly parallel routes) had gone a long way towards getting Victorian railway companies into financial problems in the first place. In the twentieth century the rationalisation of railway routes increasingly meant that the competitive challenge was between the industry as a whole and other forms of transport, most obviously road.

The reasons for a lack of intra-railway competition today are not hard to find. The fact that all trains must run along a fixed track, to which access is controlled, is one. The fact that most journeys can only be accomplished along one such track is another. Pick any city in Britain and decide to travel from it to any other, and there is generally only one way to go, unless time and money are no object. The network today is very nearly a natural monopoly for those who wish to travel by rail between two places, offering one viable service option in each case, and competing with road and (for business passengers over a few longer journeys) air travel.

There are a few exceptions. You can travel between London and Birmingham on the West Coast mainline from Euston or on the Chiltern line from Marylebone. Since the latter is a much slower line, single-tracked in places, this does not provide the basis for a real competition for the custom of the majority of passengers travelling the whole journey.

Either the East or the West Coast main lines will take you from London to Glasgow. And there is a choice of ways to commute between London and Southend, or between Liverpool and Manchester. That is more or less it. Franchising has not altered this state of affairs. The former Bishop of Birmingham put it well at the time of privatisation: 'As for competition between franchisees, what does it matter if the London-Bristol route is running faster when you want to travel from York to Edinburgh?'[1]

To return to our London-Birmingham example. You may take a train from Euston to Birmingham New Street with either the intercity franchisee (Virgin) or the suburban franchisee (Silverlink). Both, however, run on the same trackbed for the entire route. Where that route is four-tracked (two lines running in each direction), the former has priority on the fast lines, running trains non-stop between the two cities, or with only two or three halts. The suburban franchisee runs a variety of stopping services. The former therefore has an effective monopoly on those wishing to travel rapidly between the two cities, while the latter has a near monopoly on the custom of those wishing to use most intermediate stations.

Very few of the twenty-five train operators are in genuine competition with any other of them. Yet it was the myth that such competition was possible that underpinned the original Adam Smith Institute (ASI) privatisation blueprint which John MacGregor had adopted. One of the first to tacitly accept this was the author of the ASI document, Ken Irvine, who hastened to set up a company, Prism Rail, to bid for some of these monopoly franchises!

For all its rhetoric, the government of the time broadly recognised the railways' status as a natural monopoly when it came to the details of privatisation. Railtrack was created as a private monopoly owning the railway infrastructure – the largest private monopoly in the country. And the twenty-five train operating companies (TOCs) were so structured as to make genuine competition between them less than a rarity. The early idea of 'open access' onto the tracks was quickly deferred, leaving each franchisee as a local monopoly.

There is, however, even less competition than this suggests. While each franchise remains a distinct entity, there is no restriction on any company owning as many franchises as it can successfully bid for, and managing them as it will, within the terms of the franchise agreement, in relation to its other assets. Initial government guidance to the franchising authority required a spread of ownership, but this has not prevented a rapid consolidation since.

As the first round of franchises was awarded on the basis of bidding to run the route with the lowest public subsidy, this was bound to favour larger companies which could spread overheads and extract the greatest 'efficiencies' at the expense of the travelling public and employees alike.

So it has proved. Privatisation has unleashed not competition, but a new stampede towards monopolies, both those which integrate different rail franchises under one management and those which unite train and bus franchises in the same region within one company.

The latter may arguably offer benefits of integration, with bus and train operations being closely co-ordinated. In private hands, however, it also creates the danger of higher fares and diminished services.

Train operating companies

In 2001, therefore, the great bulk of rail franchises were in many fewer hands than might be supposed. While every effort has been made to revive images from the 'golden age' of rail with names like

Great Western and Great Eastern, the reality is more mundane. Britain's emerging train monopolies have ended up under the ownership of existing bus monopolies, following a number of take-overs and mergers.

Start with the National Express Group. This company is best known as the operator of the only scheduled express coach network in the country, serving 1,200 destinations. It also runs 1,800 buses in the west midlands in its Travel West Midlands operation.

This latter operation sits nicely with Central Trains, the regional train franchise also operated by National Express. Central is only one of nine TOCs currently owned by the company. Others include West Anglia Great Northern (WAGN) which, with its Stansted Express service gives National Express a near-monopoly on public transport between the fast growing airport and the capital.

The fruits of this monopoly were vividly demonstrated on Boxing Day 2000, when National Express ended all rail and coach services from the airport several hours before the last (scheduled) flights landed. Newly arrived passengers were left stranded in enormous queues for taxis, many not arriving in London until many hours later. WAGN's management has been described by one industry specialist as 'particularly dire'.[2]

National Express also runs the c2c (formerly London-Tilbury-Southend line), the Midland Mainline, ScotRail, Silverlink, the Valley Lines in south Wales, the Wales & West regional franchise and Gatwick Express. The same company further owns a big stake in the running of the Eurostar service between London, Paris and Brussels.

The group's last published interim results showed a 46.7 per cent increase in profits with a 13 per cent rise in the interim dividend to shareholders. Passengers are not likely to be as satisfied as shareholders – Silverlink, for example, has the lowest customer satisfaction rating of any TOC, the more so since it announced above-inflation fare increases in the aftermath of the Hatfield crash, when its service oscillated between the deplorable and the non-existent. Eight of its nine franchises featured in the list of the top ten highest fare increases announced in January 2001.[3]

Then there is Arriva plc. It operates around 20 per cent of London's buses and also has operations in Glasgow and Leicester. Most relevantly, however, it also runs the bus service in Liverpool, Manchester, Newcastle and Leeds, operations which dovetail with its two rail franchises – Arriva Trains Merseyside (formerly Merseyrail Electrics) and Arriva Trains Northern (formerly Northern Spirit), the regional operators in Yorkshire and the north-east at present, and the operator of Arriva transpennine. This translated into pre-tax profits of £95.2 million in 1999, with a 5 per cent increase in dividend payments. Arriva has also recently wrung a hefty 36 per cent subsidy increase out of the Strategic Rail Authority for operating Northern Spirit.[4]

The Go-Ahead Group holds the Thames Trains franchise, running suburban and local services out of London's Paddington station. It is also a major bus operator in Oxford, one of its railway destinations. One of its trains was involved in the Ladbroke Grove crash of 1999 – an accident that could have been avoided had its directors invested in available train protection systems. This was neglected on grounds of expense – yet the same directors ensured that management performance bonuses were paid, with a total of £1 million going to the two most senior managers.

Thames Trains' five original directors – all middling BR managers – received £4.3 million when Go-Ahead bought the company. They had originally invested just £10,000 each, making them notable beneficiaries of the privatisation process. At the time, their franchise was still receiving £18 million a year in public subsidy.[5]

Go-Ahead also runs the Thameslink franchise, which crosses central London, linking Bedford and Luton to the north of the city with Gatwick Airport and Brighton in the south. Go-Ahead has now been selected by the Strategic Rail Authority as the preferred bidder for the South Central franchise hitherto (mis)managed by Connex, a French-owned operator which has become a byword for bad industrial relations, clapped out rolling stock and unreliable services.

The key route on this franchise is between Brighton and London's Victoria and London Bridge stations. By awarding this operation to the company that also holds the Thameslink franchise, the SRA has created a monopoly on this route in the hands of Go-Ahead. The group is also, incidentally, the bus operator in Brighton. Again, profits for the year ending July 2000 were up 8 per cent on the previous year (to over £44 million), but dividends increased by 13 per cent, to much appreciation from shareholders, no doubt.

The largest bus operator in the UK is First Group, with 10,000 vehicles and 23 per cent of the market, which runs buses in every part of the country. It, too, has become a big player in the railway industry, operating three major franchises – the Great Western from Paddington to south Wales and the west country, the Great Eastern from Liverpool Street to East Anglia and the North Western regional service. For good measure, it also runs the new Croydon Tramlink service.

Great Western was fined £1.5 million for its culpability in the Southall crash in 1997, an accident which exposed a casual attitude towards safety operations by the company: its train had started out that day with one safety system switched off and the other identified as malfunctioning.

Its directors, however, were luckier. When the company was sold to First Group the year after Southall, the eleven directors shared £23 million, with Chief Executive Brian Scott alone receiving £7 million. Another executive, Richard George, saw his £40,000 investment yield a return of almost £3 million, twice the fine levied after Southall, for which it was recommended by British Transport Police that Mr George be prosecuted (a recommendation not accepted by the Director of Public Prosecutions).[6]

First Group profits for the year 2000 were over £190 million, up from £145 million in 1999. Dividends increased, too, from 7.3 pence per share to 8.5 pence.

Stagecoach plc runs the South West Trains franchise, with services from London Waterloo to Surrey, Hampshire and Dorset. As well as twelve major bus operations around the country, it also owns 49 per cent of Richard Branson's Virgin Trains. Dividend payments rose by 8.3 per cent, on profits of £126.6 million, in the six months to the end of October 2000.

Virgin is notorious as the operator of the West Coast mainline service and the CrossCountry service (broadly, long distance inter-city trains which do not commence or terminate in London). Virgin and Stagecoach are two of the three franchises which run trains from London to Scotland, and no inter-city railway company in the post-privatisation years has attracted more opprobrium on grounds of inefficiency and failure to meet customer service requirements.

That has not deterred Virgin/Stagecoach from bidding to run the third England-Scotland service, the East Coast Main Line franchise presently run by GNER, part of Sea Containers (rail-related profits up 27 per cent in the latest quarter). This bid was being seriously entertained (as of May 2001) by the SRA, notwithstanding the fact that it would give Virgin a monopoly on train services from London to Glasgow and Edinburgh, for example. No doubt this is a testimony to the political influence of Richard Branson, a prototype hippie entrepreneur who has sprayed the Virgin brand onto everything from trains to cola to mobile phones and is a personal friend of Tony and Cherie Blair.

As things stand, just four groups – National Express, First Group, Connex and Virgin/Stagecoach – control 70 per cent of the TOC's total franchise revenue. The detail of this map will change as some of the franchises are re-drawn or consolidated; some of the companies listed above are hoping to snatch franchises from their rivals as they come up for auction once more. However, it will not change the broad fact that privatisation has created half a dozen or so public transport monopolies which compete very little with each other but occupy a commanding position vis-à-vis the passenger.[7]

Freight

Nor has competition fared much better in the rail freight sector. The original Conservative plan – to create three separate, regionally based trainload freight companies to handle the great bulk of this business – fell at the first hurdle. It was found that there was an insufficient capital market for such businesses, so all three were sold to the same bidder, US company Wisconsin Central, which consolidated the three as the English Welsh and Scottish railway (EWS). This has a near monopoly of most categories of freight haulage. Freightliner operates much of the container business. A few smaller operators serve specialist markets and one or two new companies have dipped their toes in the water, since 'open access', an idea long abandoned for the passenger railway, still prevails in the freight sector.

Track and stations

At the centre of the structure of the privatised railway there is the mother of all monopolies, Railtrack plc. This was privatised in the manner familiar to the Thatcher–Major years, via a public share offering. To encourage interest in the sell-off, it had much of its debt written off by the taxpayer, and was structured so as to give it a position of great power relative to the train operating companies, a position it has shamelessly abused ever since.

As with other privatisations of the time, many of the shares in Railtrack were initially held by small investors. This, however, has changed, a factor which should be borne in mind when considering the issue of restoring the company to public ownership. In 1996, 58 per cent of shares were held by small shareholders, the rest by financial institutions. By 2000, the situation had been reversed. 57 per cent of the company is now owned by UK-based financial institutions, and 25 per cent by those based overseas, with only 18 per cent still in the hands of individual shareholders.

75 per cent of the company is owned by institutions or people with more than 100,000 shares in it. And they have done very well out of the investment. Railtrack's dividend per share has risen from 22 pence (1997) to 24 pence (1998) to 26.3 pence in 1999, a 9.5 per cent increase 'in line with the company's progressive dividend policy'

– money that comes straight out of the investment pot. In the wake of the Hatfield crash, in the midst of the chaos, the Railtrack board announced a further 5 per cent increase in the interim dividend payable to shareholders. In total, Railtrack shareholders have received dividends of £572 million since 1996.

Profits in 1999 rose to £430 million – not bad for a private monopoly subject to regulation, and receiving much of its income indirectly from public subsidy. Money paid by taxpayers to the train operating companies and then handed on by them to the track monopoly in access charges is the bedrock of Railtrack's finances. This subsidy is currently running at a rate of 1.3 billion pounds a year, out of a total access charge income of £2.3 billion. Money for major investments comes directly from government as well, on top of the indirect subsidies. And, as we shall see when considering the post-Hatfield crisis, whenever Railtrack hits hard times, it simply holds out the begging bowl for more, knowing that the government cannot afford to let it go under.

For even the must devoted disciple of free-market capitalism, it's an unattractive sight. A private monopoly largely funded through massive public subsidy, paying out increasing dividends to shareholders while pleading that rising debts require further public money or an abandonment of its investment plans. Either that or bankruptcy.

Rolling stock

If shareholders in the TOCs and in Railtrack have clearly done very well, they may still look with envy at the managers who borrowed a little money to buy the rolling stock leasing companies (which own the engines and carriages) when they were privatised. These are the fattest cats in the story of the privatised railway.

British Rail's rolling stock was divided during the approach to privatisation more or less equally between three companies specially created for the purpose – Eversholt, Porterbrook and Angel Trains, each named after the streets in which they were originally head-quartered.

At privatisation, the first two companies were sold to management buy-outs, while Angel was sold to a consortium of engineering and financial companies, among whom was former BR manager John Prideaux. In total, the three sales netted about £1.8 billion for what was around half of the British railway industry's assets at the time of privatisation.

Then, from the point of view of the City institutions, the fun began. First to go was Porterbrook, sold on by its management buy-out team to Stagecoach just a few months later – for a gain of just under £300 million. Eversholt lasted under its buy-out managers until 1997 when it was sold to the HSBC banking group for a premium of £208 million. Finally, Angel was sold to the Royal Bank of Scotland for £1.1 billion – 58 per cent higher than the GRSH consortium had paid for it two years earlier.[8]

This set of transactions made some very middling British Rail managers very rich. The Department of Transport, in its 1993 paper on privatising the ROSCOs, had noted the government's belief that 'there is much to be gained from transferring the provision of rolling stock to the private sector as quickly as possible'. Certainly, much has been gained: Mr Prideaux made £15 million personally from the sale of Angel Trains to the bankers. Sandy Anderson scooped up £36 million for the re-sale of Porterbrook after a few months in charge, and an initial investment of £150 million, while three other executives shared £30 million between them. Andrew Jukes, Chief Executive, made nearly £16 million on an investment of £110,000 (most of it borrowed) through the privatisation of Eversholt, two of his co-directors making £11.6 million each on an investment of £80,000 apiece.[9]

In the whole sorry saga of railway privatisation, these are possibly the biggest winners of all, the men who made most from doing least, taking home a fortune through speculation in the sale of public assets. Even Tony Blair, neither friend of public ownership nor foe of the fat cat, declared this proceeding 'entirely unjustified' and an example of 'profiteering'.

It was also an example of a casual Conservative disregard for stewardship of the public finances. The huge mark-up that accured over a matter of months must indicate that the original sale price, of the assets involved was far too low. This, in turn, must have reflected government determination to push on with privatisation (at a time when Labour was still threatening to reverse the whole sell-off on coming to office) by selling off public assets on the cheap.

Porterbrook was sold on again by Stagecoach in April 2000 for a further premium to Abbey National, thereby placing all three ROS-COs in the hands of large banks. The biggest loser has clearly been the taxpayer, robbed of £900 million to the advantage of a handful of BR managers and some large financial institutions.

Infrastructure companies

British Rail's infrastructure maintenance business was split into thirteen different companies (to be known as INFRACOs) at the time of privatisation. The new subsidiaries were mainly regionally based. Again, a series of take-overs has consolidated the business into fewer hands, with familiar names. Seven companies control the entire market, with GTRM (part of construction servicing giant Carillion), Balfour Beatty, Jarvis and First Engineering the biggest players. These four companies between them control over 80 per cent of the maintenance and renewals market. In each case, railway business is just part of a larger range of construction and civil engineering activities.[10]

Their work is assigned on contract by Railtrack: each will be given a particular line for a particular time, a system designed to generate conflict according to one trade publication:

> [contractors] have complained to the regulator about not having enough time to submit quality tenders, poorly specified workloads, and an over-emphasis on price. Wholesale changes to track renewal programmes after the contract has been awarded have wasted resources and money. Even worse for them, while contractors are expected to bear substantial financial risk, heavy fines are imposed if trains are delayed.[11]

The system is designed to minimise the time when track is put out of operation for engineering work – known as 'possessions' in the industry. Railtrack's finances, based on access charges paid by train operators, obviously depend on train running. When they cannot secure that access, Railtrack must compensate them, giving the track company a vested interest in keeping closures due to engineering work to a minimum, and re-opening lines as fast as possible. Even if the lines are in a poor state, leading to unreliable service, Railtrack can still claim back some of the money it has to pay train operators in fines levied on contractors!

Railtrack's determination to force down the price of maintenance work as far as possible, to the advantage of its own shareholders, has been compounded by sheer negligence – the company does not even hold a central register of its assets. Despite years of pressure from the regulator, Railtrack remains in a position of blissful ignorance regarding both the extent and the state of the assets it owns, unless they are earmarked for lucrative property development. This became all too obvious in the wake of the Hatfield crash.

This is not to suggest that the Infracos deserve too much sympathy, though. These, after all, were the firms who had been quietly canvassing the possibility of widening their profit margins when the quality of maintenance work and control came under the spotlight after the Hatfield disaster.

The chain of command does not end there, however. These contractors themselves subcontract out the supply of much of the labour to do this work. Jimmy Knapp, the general secretary of RMT, the largest railway union, told the Cullen enquiry into railway safety that he estimated there were perhaps a thousand firms involved on the railways in this way.

Perhaps this is the peculiar 'genius' of the form of privatisation imposed by the Major government. It has entrenched a system of competition through contracts which creates little but damage, with costs cut to the bone in vital areas of work. At the same time it exchanged a public-service monopoly for private sector ones in situations where greater responsiveness to the consumers' requirements was desirable – in the running of the trains themselves.

Contracts and regulators

Two things hold this rickety structure together, in place of the operational unity of the old British Rail, or even the vertically integrated monopolies of pre-nationalisation days: legal contracts and regulation.

The former impose a dense network of incentives and penalties for each and every bit of the industry. Railtrack charges train operating companies fees for access to the network. These fees do not increase in proportion to the investment that would be required to upgrade the lines to allow greater access, so Railtrack has little interest in carrying out such infrastructure upgrades in order to permit more trains to run. Effectively, the buck for any major new investment is therefore passed back to the taxpayer in large measure.

As already noted, if Railtrack cannot for any reason allow the contractually guaranteed access to the railway, it has to pay a penalty to the operators. This, of course, makes closing parts of a line for necessary maintenance work expensive, and Railtrack is therefore reluctant to do it unless absolutely necessary. It is for this reason that early in its existence, the infrastructure monopoly instituted a policy of 'sweating the assets' – extending the life of signals and track beyond their allotted span until they showed actual signs of deterioration.

If, however, a train causes a delay on the line, then the operating company is responsible for paying a charge to Railtrack, which may pass all or some of it on to other operators inconvenienced by the delay. A rambling and complicated system devised by accountants and operated by IT specialists (to the profit, ultimately, of lawyers) has been created to track train movements – not in order to improve performance, but to monitor and attribute the responsibility for delays. It goes by the name of TRUST (Train Running System), and its oppressive workings surface time and again in conversations with railway workers at the front line.

TRUST consists of 2,900 'reporting points' and 1,300 'delay attribution points', which pin the blame for every missed minute in timetable performance on Railtrack, one or more TOCs or other elements in the privatised system. In addition, there are 500 'contract monitoring points' and 366 'passenger charter monitoring points'. 86 per cent of this vast data collection exercise is done automatically, with the rest 'captured manually', in the words of one authority, in signal boxes – a considerable burden to signallers.[12]

The passengers have not benefited from this tortuous system. Indeed, through its basic principle of instituting a pass-the-blame-for-cash-prizes culture, it has led to one of privatisations most infuriating absurdities – train connections not being held. Under the public service ethos, if Train A was running ten minutes late, Train B would be held at the destination station to take on board those passengers from Train A who wished to travel onwards. Under the private profit dispensation, Train B's operator would face fines, so away it goes and woe betide any public-spirited Railtrack signaller who tries to delay its departure and therefore permits the TOC to make a claim against Railtrack. For the passengers, a ten-minute delay may become one of an hour or more, until the next train on Train B's route departs.

The contractual relationship between Railtrack and its infrastructure maintenance and renewal contractors is open to more conventional monopoly abuses. There are, as noted, a handful of companies involved in this field, bidding for work from Railtrack, which has the power to condemn the entire railway divisions of these businesses to oblivion, should it so wish.

Railtrack has behaved as the textbooks on the economics of monopoly would lead one to expect. It systematically drives down the price of the contracts, divulging the details of a first bidder's tender to a second bidder, and inviting them to undercut it. This may then be repeated with a third company, until the work is contracted out for an impossibly cheap rate. Such a practice can, in theory, only impact on the quality of work carried out, and so it has proved in practice. Railway maintenance has been done too late, on the cheap and in a hurry when finally undertaken – something Railtrack would, of course, blame on the INFRACOs, which it has accused of operating like a 'cartel'! Seldom has a darker pot abused a dirtier kettle.

The problems this causes have been exacerbated by Railtrack's laxity in monitoring contracts. This was first publicly noted in 1997 after a goods train derailed at Bexley in Kent on account of rotting sleepers on the track bed, but little changed thereafter. Neither engineering skills nor contract control were Railtrack's forte, although it excelled at turning railway stations into shopping malls.

Cut-backs are also forced on the train operating companies – those running the less glamorous franchises in particular. Faced with the requirement for a declining public subsidy over the terms of the franchise, the pressure is on to squeeze more and more passengers onto their trains, or reduce the service to the minimum level mandated by their franchise agreement.

For example, when Prism Rail (now part of the National Express Group) was the operator of the Wales & West franchise, it decided to cut services on one route in Devon from the eleven a day run by BR to the minimum seven provided for in its agreement with the franchising authority. Devon County Council had to supply a further subsidy to Prism to prevail upon it to up the number of trains to nine a day.

This baroque system is crowned by three different regulators (four, when the government itself is included). One, the Railways Inspectorate (now part of the Health and Safety Executive) is responsible for monitoring safety standards and investigating accidents. A second, the Office of the Franchising Director, has now had its functions absorbed into the Strategic Rail Authority (SRA). This body draws up franchise agreements, allocates them to bidders, monitors their performance and disburses around the private industry the considerable sums of public money still invested in the running of the railway. The SRA now has the power to fine train operators for performance failures.

The Office of the Rail Regulator (ORR) issues licences to operate to Railtrack, TOCs, rail freight companies and others. It has the power to fine Railtrack or even to strip it of its licence – although this is an entirely empty threat unless privatisation is to be abandoned, since there is no other company in the field which could take the licence over. The ORR also monitors the access agreements between the track monopoly and the train operators, and is supposed to ensure that the whole industry operates to the general benefit of the public, loosely in line with such guidance as it may receive from government. The ORR does not, however, regulate the contracts of the rolling stock leasing companies.

It remains a matter of debate as to whether this elaborate regulatory environment is part of the problem. It would certainly seem to be no part of the solution, if for no other reason than that there is, at present, no sign of a solution to be part of. What is clear is that it has to date failed to ensure the safe, efficient, service-oriented railway promised at the time of privatisation. In part this may be to do with a general problem of regulation of private business – once responsibility to shareholders is enshrined as the priority, and the stock market becomes the measure of success, regulation becomes ineffective unless directed at very specific objectives.

For example, every time the present Rail Regulator, Tom Winsor (one of the lawyers employed in 1993–95 to devise the system in the first place), criticises Railtrack, or levies a fine on it for its failure to meet required improvements, the monopoly's share price falls away, making it still harder for the company to raise funds for investment. While the SRA may be pressing Railtrack to increase investment, the rail regulator is at the same time urging it to curb costs and reduce charges to the operators.

The regulators have also established a bureaucratic regime more slow moving and obstructive than anything a nationalised industry managed. Because Railtrack is heavily regulated, any development touching on it, and most railway developments do, has to be referred to the regulator. Decisions which were reached swiftly under BR now drag on for months or years as everyone's contractual interest is considered and reconciled and the legal profession waxes fat.

The balance sheet

This system and structure has now been in place for more than five years, so it is not too soon to attempt some judgement as to how the 'new railway' has performed with 'market-oriented thrust' replacing the more mundane objective of 'running trains' as the *raison d'être* of the whole enterprise.

The defenders of privatisation, the few that are left, rest their case on the claims that passenger numbers and freight tonnage carried have both increased considerably since the demise of BR. Both claims are certainly true. Passenger kilometres travelled have risen from 30 billion in 1995/96 to 38.5 billion in 1999/2000. This, however, overstates the extent of the improvement since privatisation, since 34.3 billion passenger kilometres were travelled under BR as recently as 1988/89. Total passenger journeys were 947 million in 1999/2000, up from 761 million in 1995/96.[13]

It is very far from clear, however, that any of this growth can really be attributed to privatisation. Indeed, given the unremittingly negative publicity concerning the punctuality, efficiency and cleanliness of the train service under private ownership, it would be surprising if this were so. In fact, train travel tends to track economic growth as a whole fairly closely, and the years since privatisation have seen consistent stable growth in the UK economy, whereas the last years of BR were years of recession. General economic conditions have a particular impact on the number of longer distance, and hence more expensive, rail journeys undertaken.

It is also very likely that train travel would have increased in any event given the increasing congestion on the roads. While the

Thatcher–Major administrations built roads as fast as they privatised industries, this programme failed to alleviate the congestion. In and around London, in particular, road travel has become increasingly unpleasant, slow and environmentally and individually debilitating. This alone would lead to increasing commuting by rail. Even here, the number of journeys made by holders of season tickets, is only now back to the level it stood at in the late 1980s, suggesting that privatised railways have not appeared as an attractive alternative to crowded roads for many people.

Many of the same considerations apply to freight haulage. Whoever owns the railways, they can be an increasingly desirable option, if operating properly, to having one's goods stuck in endless traffic jams. Freight moved has increased to 18.4 billion tonne kilometres in 1999/2000, as against 13.3 billion in 1995/96. Again, the former figure is only very slightly more than the 18.1 billion moved in 1988/89, before economic recession kicked in.

Freight levels were also artificially depressed in the last years of BR by the management's determination, at the insistence of government, to drive away as many customers as possible and shrink the business rapidly to the point where it might make a profit.

As Julia Clarke, the present Head of Freight at the Strategic Rail Authority put it:

> Customers failing to deliver the volume needed to fill daily trains were faced with dramatic price increases, in at least one case of more than 200 per cent ... Terminal operators were faced with service reductions or complete withdrawals of service and a number closed, others went into liquidation or withdrew entirely from the rail freight business. 'Exit pricing'

became a term used to describe the process whereby operationally inconvenient business was priced off the network with
unreasonable price increases.[14]

BR was thus already being made to work, in relation to freight, to
a privatisation-style mandate to make as much money as it could
whatever the social consequences. It is not surprising that the industry
has had nowhere to go but up, and the volume increases should be
seen in that context. Even the passenger network had been managed
for contraction for more than a generation before privatisation and
the Major government assumed that growth would be unlikely. The
private industry, therefore, took advantage of a long pent-up potential for more intensive railway use, rather than being the cause of it.
Had the iron grip of the Treasury been relaxed, British Rail might
well have developed in the same way as many other state-run
railways in Europe.

A second argument used by the pro-privatisation lobby is that at
least turning the whole industry over to the private sector has saved
taxpayers' money. Once again, the facts are a good deal more
ambivalent. In the four post-privatisation years for which figures are
available, total government support for the rail industry has totalled
£5,889 million. For the four previous years, it totalled £5,926 million,
an insignificant difference. Government support for each of the last
three years has been greater than for any year before 1991/92 –
although then, at least, all the cash that went into the industry stayed
there, while much of the taxpayers' money today finds its way
indirectly into shareholders' bank accounts.

The Labour government has committed itself, at least on paper, to
an ambitious programme of railway expansion over the next ten

years, nearly half of which is to be publicly funded. Welcome as this is, it seems clear that the taxpayer is going to enjoy no relief as a result of privatisation, since Railtrack's worsening balance sheet means that all major investment projects will have to be funded through the Treasury, just as in the days of nationalisation.

The public may also have formed the impression that investment in the industry has soared since privatisation. This misunderstanding arises in part from the various submissions made in the course of the bidding process for franchises, and Railtrack's own annual network management statement. All of these documents are replete with outlines of costly (and often competing) investment schemes. Huge sums of money are bandied about. Much of this is speculative, however, consisting of 'wish-lists' of projects, only a few of which will actually be realised. Railtrack's inability to accurately forecast the cost of major projects is already a standing joke in any case, as the ever-soaring cost of the improvements to the West Coast mainline (now nearly three times the original estimates) shows.

The actual investment record is a good deal more prosaic. Expressed in constant (1998/99) prices, investment in the railways slumped catastrophically from £1,707 million in 1992/93, the year privatisation was announced, to £1,330 the next year and £1,185 two years after that, in 1995/96. 1996/97 saw only the slightest improvement. The process of selling off the railway was accompanied by a disastrous drop in new money going into the industry. Here, without a doubt, are the roots of many of the infrastructure and rolling stock problems besetting the network, problems for which the privatisation process, even before the final formal transfer of ownership, must bear the responsibility.

Over the last three years, it is true, investment has increased once more, to £2,182 million in 1999/2000, expressed in constant prices. However, this is only making good the backlog created by the sell-off years and is not evenly distributed across the network, with the more profitable franchises on higher profile routes securing the lion's share. £1,418 billion represents the government support for the industry in the same accounting year, leaving a net private sector investment of £764 million.

To set against this, one should also consider how much money leaks out of the industry in payments to shareholders, 'fat cat' emoluments for managers, lawyers' fees and other costs associated with the administration of the conflict-by-contract system. It is impossible to be precise about all these figures. Railtrack excepted, the major railway businesses are part of larger companies. While profits can be broken down between divisions, one cannot easily attribute portions of dividend payments in the same way. Taking Railtrack's dividend payments as a starting point (nearly £600 million over five years), however, it would not seem unreasonable to assume that perhaps as much as one third of the private sector investment figure should be discounted against payments to shareholders and to senior management over and above what they might have received under British Rail.

In the context of these amounts (and, indeed, almost any other context) the gains of up to £17 million pocketed by each of the directors of the ROSCOs when they were sold on to the banks are also significant. £17 million could, for example, have funded a new freight terminal at Aberdeen, with money to spare, or the refurbishment programme at Cardiff Central station, and could have paid several times over for a plan to improve suburban train services in Edinburgh, to take but three improvements suggested in Railtrack's

Network Management Statement for 2000. Or it could buy six new trains for South West Trains, or open four new stations. The investment opportunity for a few has been a lost opportunity for a better railway for the many.[15]

As for punctuality and performance on the passenger railway, it was deteriorating on the great majority of franchises even before the Hatfield disaster and the subsequent meltdown of the service. Of the six high-speed franchises, only Virgin CrossCountry showed any improvement at all on the latest year-on-year comparisons, and that was from an extremely low level to begin with (fewer than 80 per cent of trains arriving on time).

All of the suburban franchises within and around London showed a worsening performance, while just two of the ten regional franchises improved their record. Notoriously elastic punctuality figures were likewise somewhat worse in 1999/2000 than they had been two and three years earlier, although slightly ahead of pre-privatisation levels. The post-Hatfield figures were, of course, still worse, with punctuality and reliability still at all-time lows more than six months after the accident.

The official figures mask, however, the full extent of the problem. Trains arriving up to ten minutes late may, under some circumstances, be counted as 'on time'. Even worse, whole days can be declared 'void' from the point of view of record-keeping if disruption on the relevant part of the network was substantial. Virgin claimed 137 such void days in one year alone!

One can go further, beyond the realm of statistics alone, in examining the record of the privatised industry. Passengers have had to tolerate a level of inconvenience and discomfort which cannot easily be captured in figures:

— The filthy state of the rolling stock on many franchises, of which Connex South-Central was merely the worst example.

— Chronic overcrowding on many commuter routes, often due to a lack of investment in new rolling stock.

— The non-interchangeability of tickets between companies running on the same route, leaving WAGN customers forbidden to board GNER trains from Peterborough to Kings Cross, for example.

— The fact that Virgin will only serve meals to first-class passengers on its West Coast mainline trains, depriving 'standard' passengers of one of the occasional pleasures of long-distance rail travel. For the rest, buffet cars remain the only option, places where improvements in the quality of the fare have lagged far behind increases in the fares.

— The bewildering array of prices offered for the same journey, where a difference of a day in booking a ticket can make a difference of over £100 in the price on some inter-city routes, all in the name of 'revenue maximisation' on each train. According to the most recent *OAG Rail Guide*, the network now offers the following tickets: Standard Open Return, Standard Day Return, APEX return, Bargain Return, cheap day return, DAYPEX return, Network Awaybreak Return, Super Advance Return, Supersaver Return, Saver Return, Virgin Value 14-Day Advance Return, Virgin Value 3-Day Advance Return, and Virgin Value 7-Day Advance Return. And these are only the tickets relating to standard class return journeys.[16]

This confusing and avaricious pricing is surely deterring many would-be rail users – I recall discovering that it was cheaper to stay in a decent hotel in Manchester overnight than to take the only

Virgin train from London which could get me there in time for a 9.30 meeting. Had I been prepared to arrive 40 minutes late for the meeting, my train fare would have been £80 cheaper!

Try to get this explained, and you will find yourself speaking to harassed staff at call centres who lack the basic operating or geographical knowledge to efficiently process enquiries, even assuming the lucky caller gets through – and you can't ring your local station for information any more. That station may often be unstaffed and therefore unsafe as well.

Then there is the management acumen of South West Trains, which made so many train drivers redundant that its scheduled services were left in tatters, yet which hired whole platoons (up from 100 to more than 400) of new 'revenue protection officers' to detect fare-dodgers on non-existent trains. SWT has had its franchise extended nevertheless.

To set against this, we have some newly liveried trains, matching newly costumed employees, and a range of exciting retail opportunities at large stations, offering the chance to shop around for socks, CDs and cosmetics while waiting for the local monopoly's train to arrive.

Yes, there have been some new stations opened (mostly paid for by local authorities), and some new lines constructed or restored to use. However, from any reasonable reading of the industry, it is very hard to attribute these gains to privatisation, or the franchising/regulatory regime which props it up. All of these improvements have depended in whole or part on public subsidy, much as in the days of British Rail.

Investing in the transformation of a public-service into a private-profit, publicly subsidised lottery has been immensely advantageous to railway shareholders. The gains for passengers and the community as a whole are, at the very least, much more elusive. The most that can be said for the last ten years on Britain's railways is that they have seen a fairly well managed but declining industry turned into a spectacularly badly managed but expanding one, leaving a trail of enraged passengers and newly minted millionaires in its wake.

And that is before one turns to the question of safety and the impact of privatisation on that most fundamental question. Railways have long been by far the safest form of land transport, in part due to the absolute priority given to safe operation by generations of railway workers and managers. It has taken privatisation to call the fundamental safety of Britain's railways into question.

3

Three Hundred Pieces of Rail

It's not often you get all the bits of the one hundred piece railway industry in one room together. But on October 18 2000, employees of train companies, maintenance firms, Railtrack and engineering companies, from consultants to conductors, all gathered in Central Hall, Westminster, to discuss employee perspectives on rail safety.

The seminar was held under the auspices of Lord Cullen's enquiry into rail safety (following his investigation into the Ladbroke Grove crash), to complement the formal hearings. The timing was tragically appropriate. Just the day before, the Hatfield derailment had occurred, killing four passengers and plunging the industry into the greatest safety crisis in its history.

Like so much that relates to safety and the privatised railway, the seminar came too late. However, given the record of the industry over the preceding several years, had it been held at the birth of the privatised railway, had its conclusions been written in burning letters yards high in front of every company headquarters, it's hard to imagine that much notice would have been taken.

Nevertheless, as a distillation of the wisdom of the people who work on the railways – the people privatisation was supposed to shunt aside in favour of marketing and financial high-flyers – the report on the seminar, prepared by the secretariat to the Cullen Enquiry, can hardly be bettered. It was a bitter portrait of the consequences of fragmentation, commercial rivalry and performance-driven (i.e. profit-driven, in this context) business:

> Privatisation has created a big cultural change. There is now little inter-linking of culture from one company to another. There has been a loss of comradeship between drivers, signal-men, cleaners etc. There is no longer a sense of working together. Questions of delays and attribution of blame strengthen the divide. This has led to a lack of confidence in others. No one is encouraged to discuss someone else's prob-lem, or volunteers or shares information . . .
>
> There is also a fear of losing one's job. Prior to privatisation there was a massive shedding of jobs and this increased stress levels on the staff. Since privatisation some employees have been 'reduced' to contractor status, thereby feeling less secure. There has been a fairly widespread loss of confidence in local and middle management . . . local managers appear to be more concerned with budgetary requirements, and new management structures appear to have been created to cope with perform-ance and financial penalties . . .
>
> Pressure to meet performance requirements is not new, but has intensified since privatisation . . . Whilst this may lead to a misconception that performance is a higher priority than safety, it is not. However, when performance targets are not met, there is pressure on employees to work less safely . . . There is also

pressure felt as to whether one should, or should not, report faults. Rectifying faults causes delays to services. What may be seen as excessive fault-reporting can result in disciplining . . .

Staff are frightened of reporting slight incidents of a non-serious nature, as they get pulled in by their supervisor, asked to fill out a form and sometimes get disciplined . . .

Another area of concern is the excessive hours worked by many sub-contractors, in contravention of the Hidden [the report into the Clapham Junction crash of 1988] requirements. Examples were quoted where contractors were working different shifts in different parts of the country, involving excessive travelling times which are not seen as part of the working day . . .

A major hole in the industry safety structure is the lack of quality control. It was said that there is an appalling lack of understanding of how work should be done, and this has led to shoddy workmanship . . . Maintenance levels are thought to have dramatically reduced. The emphasis is now on reactive or breakdown maintenance rather than preventative maintenance. There are inadequate checks on the quality and standard of work performed . . .[1]

Reading the report of the seminar, one is struck by the fact that were any other industry or company run in this fashion, it would be on the point of collapse. As it happens, on that very day, the private railway industry arrived right at that point.

Safety warnings

The Hatfield accident finally crystallised every concern about safety on the railways, concerns which had been growing with each year that had passed since privatisation. The employee seminar – itself the result of an independent enquiry into previous disasters, rather than an initiative from within the industry itself – was a day too late. But the industry had had plenty of previous warnings over the preceding years. The determination of each company to fight its own commercial corner, and the inadequacy of the statutory bodies responsible for monitoring safety (the Railways Inspectorate was described at the seminar as 'too interested in the paper audit trail rather than whether everybody is working safely') meant that little more than lip service was paid to addressing these concerns.

Nothing said at the employee seminar should have come as news to Railtrack in particular. The track monopoly had been given ample warning about safety on the network it manages. It was warned, in fact, by . . . itself.

Railtrack's Safety and Standards Directorate was established to monitor and enforce compliance with safety procedures throughout the industry. Its main function was to review on an annual basis the 'safety cases' which every passenger franchise and freight company, as well as many other concerns, had to prepare.

However, as a one-off, a team from the Directorate was turned loose on Railtrack itself early in 1999, before the accidents at Ladbroke Grove and Hatfield. The report the safety auditors compiled on their own employers' practices did not make comfortable reading – so much so that the audit was never released to the public and Railtrack itself did nothing about it. But it foretold almost everything that was to come to pass.

The report, a copy of which was passed to the author, is worth quoting. Bear in mind that everything in it was read by Railtrack management months before accidents which were to cause thirty-five deaths and the highest levels of disruption in the railway network's history.

The report found 'significant non-compliance' with industry safety standards, even a 'culture of non-compliance'. More specifically, the report warned that 'the checks carried out on contractors activities are insufficient' while on the critical issue of passing signals at danger, 'differing interpretations' were applied by managers in different parts of the company.

'Track maintenance', the Railtrack team found, 'has not been shown to be effectively carried out. The application of proper standards and levels of track maintenance by Railtrack's contractors could not be demonstrated.' The report also noted that 'the incidence of broken rails is increasing. Improved data is required to determine causation and take effective preventative action.'

The underlying causes of the subsequent disasters are clearly presaged here. But, when it came to discussing what should be done about the report, nothing ensued beyond a row between senior managers, which led to the audit being put to one side. The report's existence proves one thing, however: Railtrack knew the risks which were being run.

Before looking at the safety record of the privatised industry as a whole, however, it does need to be acknowledged that, as with any form of transport, no system can make rail travel perfectly safe. This was tragically demonstrated by the Selby accident in February 2001 when an express train collided with a car which had driven off a motorway, and then hit an oncoming freight train, with the loss of ten lives as a result. A series of tragic coincidences turned a minor road accident into a major railway catastrophe.

In fact, railways remain the safest form of land transport available. A bad year for deaths on the rails is still likely to be better than a good week on the roads, which is one more reason to regard the then Transport Minister Lord MacDonald's advice to travellers fed up with fare increases to go back on the roads in April 2001 as irresponsible. Nevertheless, the public clearly hold the railways to a higher standard. Firstly, it is seen as a public service rather than a private concern. Secondly, as with air travel, it is a form of transport in which the passenger surrenders personal control into the hands of others when he or she embarks. People therefore expect to be protected by those operating the system of travel, whereas in a car they may be under the misapprehension that they retain a large measure of control over their fate.

That is why the safety record of the 'new railway' has come in for such damning criticism, and why people are tired of platitudes on the subject. When a very safe, essential form of transport suddenly becomes more dangerous, it is no use telling travellers that it is still less risky than alternative means of getting about. They will want to know why safety has deteriorated, and what can be done about it.

Sense about safety

Two issues need instead to be at the centre of the debate on rail safety. Firstly, accepting that while every effort must always be made to minimise human error it will still inevitably occur from time to time, why are there no systems in place to ensure that these errors do not have such terrible consequences? Secondly, is the structure of the industry such as to ensure that commercial interests do not militate against the safe operation of the system in its day-to-day running – is there a 'safety first' culture of co-operation between the different bits of the industry when it comes to these matters, or can contractual considerations take precedence in practice?

These questions strike at the heart of the privatised industry. British Rail had its shortcomings, and it was far from immune from pressure arising out of financial considerations in the operation of the railway. Nevertheless, it generally had in place the best safety systems technically available at the time. Lessons learned from accidents were swiftly and uniformly applied, without fear that the costs of such improvements might be unacceptable to vested interests. And its culture, formed over many years, put safety first – which means that there were no institutional, contractual or commercial considerations which could lead to delays or half measures in introducing safety systems or procedures. This system was staffed by an integrated workforce, bonded by a culture of co-operation in working for one railway.

This culture in some ways explained what was often misinterpreted as 'poor service' by passengers. For example, a British Rail driver had the right not to take out a train with any fault on it, a strict procedure which sometimes led to cancellations or delays. It is true that, in its last years, under the intense financial pressures applied by the Conservative government to make privatisation more attractive to investors, the situation had already started to deteriorate. But BR's safety record was, generally, exemplary. The last fatalities attributable to a broken rail, for example, had been in 1967.

Even at the time of privatisation, many people questioned whether the privatised industry would retain British Rail's high safety standards. Any number of voices questioned the bland assurance in the white paper, repeated *ad nauseam* by ministers, that safety would not be compromised by the break-up of BR and its transfer to private ownership.

The most telling warnings came from inside the industry itself. A special report compiled by ex-BR senior managers was published in June 1993. Using tragically prescient words, the report warned: 'Safety needs clear direct lines of command. The new organisation does not provide this.' And: 'There will be pressure on Railtrack to contain its costs. Who will ensure that Railtrack carries out its very expensive responsibilities for validating and monitoring safety? 'Who guards the guards?''

The same report also warned of the consequences for safety of having so many experienced railway managers leave the industry at once and, referring to the fragmentation of the network into around 100 different companies, pointed out: 'This will cause literally thousands of legal key interfaces with severe safety validation problems'.[2]

The ex-BR executives listed several prerequisites for high standards of safety. It reads like a list of omissions by the privatised industry: Infrastructure 'designed and installed to a high standard', adequate and well trained staff, 'investment in equipment specifically designed to avoid accidents', effective 'supervision and monitoring of operations'. And in the summer of 1995, a leaked letter from Railtrack's safety chief highlighted the possibility of 'a major disaster some very short time in the future'.[3]

A further leaked document prepared by the head of operations in

Railtrack's Safety and Standards Directorate in 1996 revealed further that the company was in 'temporary non-compliance' with requirements for improved signalling mandated by an inquiry into a fatal accident at Glasgow four years previously, apparently for financial reasons.[4]

It requires a heroic leap of faith to imagine that the fragmented, fractious, uncooperative and often incompetent railway described in the previous chapter could maintain and develop the high safety standards of British Rail. The testimony of those who work in the industry, quoted extensively in Chapter 4, makes it clear that commercial pressures, and inter-company competition for cash ate into the safety culture of the industry at almost every turn. This can best be illustrated by looking at the three accidents which are either entirely rooted in the consequences of privatisation, or in which those consequences at the very least played a significant part.

Southall and Ladbroke Grove

In 1997, a Great Western express train collided with a freight train at Southall, west London. Seven people were killed in the collision, which had as its immediate cause the driver of the passenger train passing a signal set at danger – an event known in the industry as a SPAD.

Professor John Uff was set the task of investigating the reasons for the accident. Before he could announce his findings, however, the Southall accident was overshadowed by a crash which led to still more fatalities. In October 1999, a Thames Trains suburban service leaving Paddington station collided with another Great Western express approaching the terminus. Thirty-one people died as a result of the collision and subsequent inferno, including both train drivers.

Again, the immediate cause was swiftly established – the driver of the Thames Trains service had passed a signal set at danger, bringing it into the path of the oncoming express. It fell to Lord Cullen to investigate this accident – the Ladbroke Grove Enquiry – and, jointly with Professor Uff, to look at the whole issue of train protection.

It is important to examine a little more closely the questions of SPADs. It has been estimated that train drivers see around ten million red lights between them in the course of a year on Railtrack's network. Only a few hundred of these are passed, generally without putting anyone at risk – an extraordinarily small number given the pressure on drivers.

It is also obvious to everyone that no train driver would ever deliberately 'jump' a red light. (The opinion of *Sunday Mirror* columnist Carole Malone, who asserted that 'there is nothing to stop or punish those train drivers who ignore red lights and play fast and loose with our lives', is the ignorant exception.) It is quite different from the situation on the roads, where reckless car drivers may sometimes be tempted to ignore a red traffic light in order to make faster progress. A SPAD can lead to dismissal for a train driver and, more importantly still, it could put both driver and passengers in the gravest danger. This has been highlighted by recent allegations on London Underground that drivers were not reporting SPADs precisely because of the fear of disciplinary action.

So it can be taken for granted that train drivers will consistently endeavour to avoid passing a signal at danger. The tiny percentage of signals so passed in the course of a year testifies to this. Nevertheless, the possibility of human error can never be completely eliminated. Larry Harrison, the driver of the express train at Southall, was at a loss, finally, to explain the momentary lapse of concentration which led him to pass through signals against him.

Michael Hodder, the driver of the Thames Train unit at Ladbroke Grove was himself one of the victims of the tragedy. No case of negligence against him has come close to being established, despite various disreputable attempts in the media and at Lord Cullen's enquiry by those acting on behalf of Railtrack to impute various shortcomings to the late driver. The Health and Safety Executive's own report on the incident has found that the driver's conduct was far from being the most important reason for the crash.

Professor Uff reached the conclusion, through his examination of the Southall crash, that the privatisation and fragmentation of the industry has considerably eroded the safety culture inherited from British Rail. Few would now express a different view. After the Ladbroke Grove disaster, Gerald Corbett announced that Railtrack would henceforward 'put safety first', a pledge that carried with it the implication that other considerations had hitherto been foremost. Mr Corbett, alas, had to make the same commitment after Hatfield, a year later, which shows how much easier it is to make these statements on behalf of a profit-driven concern than to put them into practice.

The safety feature which received most attention in the wake of the Southall and Ladbroke Grove crashes was train protection systems. These are systems designed to prevent a signal passed at danger from becoming a disaster, whether the cause is driver error or some other factor. The most advanced such system in the world today is Automatic Train Protection, or ATP. Its most developed variant, now in use in parts of Europe, is known as the European Train Control System (ETCS).

In simple terms, ATP is best because it operates independently of the driver. It can itself bring a train to a halt without the driver having to do anything and it is effective at any speed reached by trains on the present network in Britain. Its installation would prevent many accidents, although it would not stop those which, like Hatfield, did not arise from the operation of the train but from the state of the track.

The basic technology of ATP has been around for over fifteen years, and is in operation in many other countries. Yet its introduction throughout the British railway system is still another eight years off at least, according to the government's timetable. The reasons for this are bound up, at every step of the way, with the privatisation process and the subsequent running of a commercially centred railway.

The introduction of ATP was first recommended by Sir Anthony Hidden in the report of his enquiry into the Clapham disaster of 1988. Thirty-five lives were lost as a result of, in essence, a signalling failure due in turn to poor maintenance work carried out by over-worked and over-tired staff, as was the norm in late 1980s British Rail. By then, the company was already strait-jacketed by government spending restrictions and drives for excessive economies in preparation for a profitable privatisation. The report by former BR managers on safety was unequivocal: 'The view of the majority of railwaymen was the Clapham accident was caused by the underlying scenario of pressure within the industry to meet ever tougher financial constraints. The picture that emerged from the Clapham accident was of an organisation at breaking point.'[5]

Since ATP would have prevented the accident, urging its earliest introduction seemed reasonable enough. The Transport Secretary at the time, Cecil Parkinson, agreed, and pledged to implement the Hidden recommendations in full, saying that 'finance will not stand in the way of the implementation of the report'. Parkinson thereby set a pattern of pledges which subsequent holders of his office were to follow. Words, alas, did not become deeds, and this too became part of the pattern.

When the time came to make good on the promise of Automatic Train Protection, Parkinson had gone and could not be held to account for his promises, there was another Transport Secretary in place and ATP was – too expensive. The logic was spelt out coolly by Railtrack's first chief executive, John Edmonds:

> In the aftermath of Clapham and the Hidden report, BR had committed itself to installing Automatic Train Protection . . . system-wide. This proved inordinately costly relative to its benefits and BR's risk-based report recommending withdrawal from this commitment was accepted by BR, Railtrack and HSE in 1994 and endorsed by government in 1995. Railtrack developed an alternative train protection strategy based on . . . measures which offer fewer safety benefits than ATP but at a much lower cost.[6]

This was accepted by the Major government because it did not wish to burden its privatisation project with costs which would make the different bits of the industry unattractive to private investors. So, for essentially commercial reasons, ATP was shelved, and a price has been paid by the passengers, if not by Railtrack, the train operators and the train leasing companies, whose shareholders have all been spared the costs of installation.

No one disputes that ETCS/ATP is the best system. It is computer-based, sending messages from trackside equipment to a computer in the cab, applying brakes automatically if pre-programmed speed limits are breached or signals disregarded. It thus requires an investment both in the infrastructure and the rolling stock but, once done, would prevent 98 per cent of accidents arising from the operation of the train. The most developed variant, ETCS, based on secure digital radio communication, would also have the important incidental benefit of increasing capacity on the railway by allowing more trains to run safely on the same track.

Instead of ATP, however, which could cost up to £2 billion to install across the whole network, the industry opted for the Train Protection and Warning System, the system referred to by John Edmonds above. A snip at just £330 million, TPWS warns drivers if they are going too fast or passing a red signal, and then applies the brakes automatically if the driver fails to take appropriate action.

However, TPWS is only effective at speeds of up to 75 miles per hour. Even enhanced versions of it only work at speeds of up to 100 mph. Moreover, it cannot be upgraded to meet the standards prevailing elsewhere on European railways, once installed.

It is therefore manifestly inferior to ATP. But a macabre calculation comes into play here. ATP would, it is argued, cost up to £14 million for each additional life it saves, far more than the usual cost-efficient limit of £2 million per life.

The justification for preferring TPWS has been that the latter can be installed faster. However, it is clear that ATP could have been installed universally long ago, had the Hidden recommendations been heeded and had the industry not been caught up in a privatisation-induced economy drive. Moreover, once TPWS has been installed, it seems unlikely that the private industry will then start all over again and re-install a more advanced safety system, be it ATP or the still more state-of-the-art ETCS. Only lavish provisions of public money will drag it kicking and screaming into the era which other European railways have long since been inhabiting.

The need for an automatic safety system has been dramatically illustrated by the accidents at Southall and Ladbroke Grove. Both would have been prevented had ATP been installed and operational. It is a particularly tragic irony that both accidents happened on the Great Western main line between Paddington and Bristol, the only high-speed route on which ATP has been installed along the track. In neither case, however, was it installed (in working order at least) on the trains travelling along it.

In the case of the Southall accident, ATP was not yet operational on the Great Western train because the driver had not been trained to use it. Moreover, the basic Automatic Warning System – a klaxon which sounds in the cab when a signal is passed at danger – was not working either, because it was broken, a failing which had been recorded by the train's previous driver but ignored by management at GWR. Great Western was fined £1.5 million once these facts came to light.

The inquiry also drew attention to inadequacies in GWR's driver-training procedures. Driver Harrison said: 'I did not realise how dangerous it was to drive a high speed train without the AWS. If I knew then what I know now, I would never have taken the train out.' Mr Harrison's apology, however, can read as if he bears more responsibility than he in fact did. The pressure to take the train out did not derive from his lack of understanding as much as from GWR's operating procedures.

It may be relevant here to recall that most train operators are now owned by bus operators. The bus industry has, since de-regulation in the 1980s, seen a considerable increase in the number of unsafe vehicles driven by inexperienced drivers unaware of the notional safety standards in force. Just as some of the worst aspects of the building-site culture have passed over into the railway maintenance operations, so some of the most deplorable practices of the bus industry may have reached the railways as well – in both cases through sharing a private owner.

It should also be noted that while the Southall accident would certainly have been prevented had ATP been working, TPWS alone would not have made any difference, since the express train was travelling at 80 miles per hour at the time of the fatal collision.

The Health and Safety Executive reports on Ladbroke Grove have been equally unequivocal: 'Had ATP been fitted and operational on the [Thames train] there would not have been a collision' and thirty-one lives would have been saved. ATP would certainly have halted the progress of the Thames train before it came into the path of the Great Western express. Thames Trains had, however, decided not to fit ATP to their trains on grounds of cost, the Cullen enquiry was told. Management vetoed plans to spend just £5 million (considerably less than the franchise's public subsidy) on safety measures, including ATP.[7]

The most comprehensive indictment of the industry's attitude towards train protection was delivered by John Hendy QC in his closing submission to the joint Cullen-Uff enquiry. Representing the

bereaved and injured of Southall and Ladbroke Grove, Mr Hendy
said:

> The bereaved and injured remain absolutely clear that Britain's
> railways must have, in the shortest time possible, Automatic
> Train Protection in its European format, ETCS. They are not
> satisfied with TPWS. They believe that Britain should never
> have gone down the road of TPWS with its dead-end tech-
> nology. Instead, a system capable of being, as it is called,
> migrated to ETCS should have been installed . . .
>
> But the bereaved and injured have been distressed to learn
> that in reality the option to stop installing TPWS now and
> instead install ETCS is to all intents and purposes closed. Yet
> all parties now accept that ETCS is the only way forward. A
> prime reason that ETCS cannot be installed immediately . . . is
> the abject failure of the industry to seize the opportunity to
> adopt a European-compatible system in 1995. Instead, and to
> allay public fears following the decision to dump ATP on cost
> grounds, Railtrack decided then to pursue TPWS, a system
> which bore no relation to the forthcoming 1996 European
> Directive on Interoperability. This was a tragic lost opportunity
> which may cost yet more lives . . .
>
> TPWS is a second-rate, stop-gap system . . . there was and is
> no sound basis for concluding that TPWS will deliver 68 per
> cent of the benefits of ATP. On the contrary, the evidence
> shows massive uncertainty . . . One study offered the conclusion
> that TPWS might save between 27 per cent and 82 per cent of
> the lives saved by ATP. Another put the range at 23 to 93 per

cent. Our analysis of the important 1998 HSE report leads to the conclusion that the effectiveness of TPWS might be somewhere around 38 per cent [of that of ATP] . . .

Until ETCS is installed and made operational, many passenger trains will continue to run at 125 miles per hour and will occasionally SPAD past a red light. It is a chilling thought that TPWS will only reduce the speed of such a train to between 105 and 109 miles per hour by the end of the standard safety overlap. The risk of high speed, catastrophic collision remains. The evidence is not compelling that TPWS+, still at an early stage of development, can become a workable system to fill the alarming gap in coverage between 74 miles per hour and 100 miles per hour . . .

The bereaved and injured have lost all confidence in the industry to implement ETCS or any other safety measure voluntarily. [They] note with despair the way in which recommendations of inquiries in the past have been disregarded . . . Ten years' further risk of high speed collisions is already much too long from the viewpoint of the bereaved and injured, but it cannot and must not grow longer.[8]

Yet ten years further risk is still the likelihood. The Cullen-Uff report set down a timetable for introducing ETCS or ATP on lines with a speed of over 75 miles an hour which will not see the work completed until 2010, although it should be introduced earlier on the East and West Coast main lines. Why can it be introduced on some lines but not others within six years? Financial considerations must be part of the reason.

Virgin Trains was the first to admit as much. Its CrossCountry franchise uses the Great Western route, where ATP is already installed on the track. Yet even after the Cullen-Uff recommendations, the company is refusing to fit the equipment to its trains. 'There is a cost implication,' a Virgin spokesman conceded.

The question crying out for an answer came from a survivor of the Ladbroke Grove crash, Pam Warren, who has since campaigned for improved rail safety. Why, she asked, 'twelve years after the Clapham Junction disaster are we still arguing about which safety system to put in?' It is a question to which neither the industry nor the politicians seem to have an adequate answer beyond 'there is a cost implication'.

Maintaining the railway

The shoddy saga of train protection systems is, however, only one of the major safety issues to arise out of the Southall, Ladbroke Grove and Hatfield accidents. Another is the condition of the railway infrastructure.

The HSE, examining the Ladbroke Grove crash, was highly critical of Railtrack for the state of the infrastructure around Paddington station and for its response to previous instances of trains passing signals at danger in the area. With masterful understatement, an HSE report on the incident in December 2000 pointed out that Railtrack had 'a complex relationship with train and station operating companies' which had 'the potential to create tension between commercial and safety considerations'.[9]

The HSE reports drew attention to the inadequate nature of the signalling and the 'fundamentally flawed' track layout in the area, not the first time that Railtrack had been made aware of these concerns. The procedure for acting on warnings about signalling and track problems was clearly found wanting.

If the Southall incident was down to inadequate train protection, and the Ladbroke Grove crash spotlighted concerns both about train protection and infrastructure management, the Hatfield accident focussed attention overwhelmingly on the latter factor. The state of the basic railway, and the relationships between its owner, Railtrack, and those it paid to maintain it – the infrastructure companies (INFRACOs) – was at the root of the disaster.

Several aspects of this are worthy of note. The first is the fact that, four years after it was sold to the private sector, Railtrack still had no grasp of the fundamental state of its assets. The only railway infrastructure the company showed a consistent interest in were those parts which could be profitably re-developed for non-railway uses. It did not, however, let this state of ignorance prevent it from disputing the rail regulator's valuation of the company when necessary!

Property development has, in fact, been Railtrack's forte. Its commercial property development portfolio is worth almost £2 billion – last year it made £135 million from rental income and £56 million from property sales. Many large rail stations have been turned into something akin to shopping malls. Visit Railtrack headquarters in front of Euston station, and the difference between the large area taken up by its property division and the considerably smaller area taken up by its infrastructure management operation is all too apparent.

Shortly before the company's privatisation, an internal company document conceded that the cost of restoring the network to a reasonable condition could be as much as £11 billion, at a time when

Railtrack was publicly stating that only about £1.4 billion would be needed. Sir George Young, the Tory Transport Secretary then charged with overseeing the final stages of privatisation, feebly alleged that 'the £11 billion came from an earlier survey which was subsequently overtaken by a later one'. Within five years, it was to become clear that even the higher figure was a very considerable under-estimate.[10]

The second aspect is that there had been an enormous shake-out of personnel in the railway maintenance sector which could not but raise safety issues. The Rail Maritime and Transport Union (RMT) estimated that permanently employed maintenance workers had fallen in number from 31,000 in 1994 to a maximum of 19,000 in 2000. They were in part supplemented by untrained (or inadequately trained) casual workers.

RMT's General secretary, Jimmy Knapp, told the Cullen enquiry that there was 'a proliferation of sub-contractors with insufficiently trained staff. Get a group of lads on a Friday night and off we go. We [experienced maintenance workers] have to look after them. We have had look-outs looking the wrong way. It's extra pressure on the professional workforce.'

A veteran of the industry and the labour movement whose deep Scottish accent had been heard arguing the trade union case throughout the campaigns against privatisation and beyond, Knapp estimated that there were between two and three thousand firms working on the railway infrastructure. He warned that the 'culture of sub-contracting has gone very deep'. Indeed, one national newspaper claimed to have got a reporter working on the line, without any qualifications, within a matter of hours.

The Guardian newspaper had identified the issue of railway maintenance as a disaster in the making early in 1998. A report focused on the huge staffing cut-backs which had been made in track maintenance since privatisation. The newspaper interviewed (anonymously) maintenance workers from three depots where aggregate staffing had been cut from 200 to 82 in the preceding four years.

One warned that 'at least fifty per cent of the track is on its last legs . . . there are accidents waiting to happen . . . some cowboy the other day forgot to put up a 20 mph restriction on a 70 mph route. How there wasn't an accident I'll never know.' Another said that 'my gut feeling is that we fly by the seat of our pants, and standards are lower. Companies are prepared to take more risks because Railtrack bullies them.'

A third worker said that 40 per cent of the track in his area needed replacing but there was no prospect of that happening for years. 'Railtrack is so pious. It . . . says that safety is paramount yet it gets really nasty if we cannot do a job on time, usually because the time we get to do it is impossible.' All the workers pointed to staff reductions and the introduction of casual and part-time workers with insufficient training as central to the deterioration.[11]

Staffing reduction has been the stock-in-trade of all newly privatised industries in Britain. New owners have found this the fastest and easiest way to boost short-term profit margins. The railways were no exception – as noted above, this led to such an extreme shortage of drivers on South West Trains, for example, that the company could not run its contractual service on one of the country's busiest routes.

However, in no other privatised industry have these staffing cuts been carried out with such apparent disregard for the safety consequences of shrinking the workforce. This despite the fact that the

Hidden report into the Clapham crash of 1988 had identified the excessive hours worked by signalling technicians as the cause.

As early as 1993, a health and safety journal was warning that extending drivers' hours was 'a likely focus for post-privatisation profit strategies' in the industry. There is, incredibly, no statutory limit on the number of hours a train driver may work, although restrictions are placed on the working day of both bus and lorry drivers. Guidelines recommend no more than 72 hours a week or 13 days out of 14! Many train operators find it cheaper to have fewer drivers and pay them overtime to run the service than to have a fully staffed complement of drivers on higher basic pay working a shorter (and safer) week.[12]

So the sweeping staffing reductions in the maintenance sector, begun under British Rail in its last days to prepare the way for privatisation and carried forward by both Railtrack and the infrastructure companies are part of an industry-wide sickness which has seen tens of thousands of experienced workers leave the railway. Railtrack has, post-Hatfield, admitted that maintenance staffing has fallen precipitately, and was forced to announce plans to re-hire 1,000 skilled workers in the aftermath of Hatfield. But no notice was taken of the warnings from the sharp end until it was too late.

Railtrack's main contractors, however, had somewhat different concerns, even if they led to the same conclusions. They were worried that the drive for greater efficiency sought by the rail regulator, reflected in demands for Railtrack to cut costs would ultimately compromise safety.

Mike Whelan, the chief executive of Balfour Beatty, the contractor responsible for the line around Hatfield, amongst other areas, warned that Railtrack was passing on the regulator's drive for economies to the INFRACOs: 'We may not be able to achieve it and consequently some people may compromise on the areas that we think are of prime importance,' he said just two months before the Hatfield crash.

The company chairman, Lord Weir, added that the efficiency targets were 'onerous, particularly having regard to the safety and performance standards required in the rail industry'. His Lordship was, on the same day, reporting a £6 million profit in his company's rail division.[13]

Independent warnings about the state of the infrastructure proliferated. In a report commissioned by the trade union TSSA, the Advanced Railway Research Centre at Sheffield University criticised Railtrack's under-investment in the network, which meant in turn that the age of its assets was rising.[14]

Finally, there had been several official warnings to Railtrack about increases in broken rails. The rail regulator had indicated 'serious concern' about the increasing number of broken rails in the network, although there had been a small reduction in the months immediately before Hatfield. Some industry sources attribute this belated improvement to the misattribution of broken rails as merely 'defective', a designation which requires less decisive action. Be that as it may, a Railtrack spokesman boasted of the improvement in the incidence of broken rails, but added 'we accept there's some more to do'. Indeed there was.

All of these chickens came home to roost in the Hatfield disaster. In November 1999, maintenance contractor Balfour Beatty warned of gauge-corner cracking (small cracks on the rail caused by the train wheel on curves in the track) on the stretch of the East Coast Main Line near Hatfield, although it appears that problems may first have been noticed the previous year. This in itself would have been an achievement, since the track inspector subsequently told the inquiry held by Railtrack's Rail Safety subsidiary that he did the inspections from a ditch by the side of the line, which meant he could not see the high rail very well. His manager for the area told the same investigation that he was 50 per cent behind in inspections because of a shortage of skilled staff.

The company recommended that re-railing be undertaken within the next six months. The job was given to Jarvis, another of the INFRACOs. There then followed a farcical series of blunders, including surveys of the wrong part of the line, missed slots to undertake the work, non-arriving and late arriving maintenance trains bearing new rails and finally delays due to a lack of skilled welders, since many subcontractors had found more remunerative work elsewhere. Once the new rails had finally been delivered, Railtrack itself displayed no great urgency about seeing Jarvis do the work. This would have been in line both with its corporate policy of 'sweating the assets' and its reluctance to incur the financial penalties (in the form of compensation to TOCs) which would follow from taking the line out of service for a period while the re-railing was undertaken.

For four months Railtrack and Jarvis argued about the timing of the work as the track eroded and decayed beneath the high-speed trains still permitted to run over it at full tilt. It was finally scheduled for November, eleven months after Balfour Beatty had definitively recommended the rail's replacement and, as it turned out, two weeks after the rail had finally shattered. The whole episode may lead to criminal charges against senior managers under corporate manslaughter legislation.

As was noted by Railtrack's own safety auditors in the report cited earlier in this chapter, the incidence of broken rails had been increasing. One possible cause for this was the decision of the Railtrack board to virtually cease the procedure of grinding rails – a universally accepted method of maintaining rails in good repair by grinding out cracks before they grow – on the grounds that it was not cost-effective.

The company had, in any case, turned its back on any hint of an 'engineering culture' in favour of Mr MacGregor's 'market-oriented thrust' – it lacked the personnel to either undertake important engineering work itself or to properly supervise, monitor and evaluate that undertaken on its behalf by other companies. To this day any engineer hired by Railtrack would have to go and work for another company to acquire the necessary qualifications to undertake railway engineering work, an astonishing position for the owner of Britain's railway infrastructure to be in.

Indeed, the entire infrastructure management system seems designed for disaster. One of Gerald Corbett's bright ideas on becoming Railtrack chief executive was to delay replacing assets like track and signalling equipment until their condition demanded it – a shift from the previous policy of replacement when the assets reached a fixed age. The main flaw in this new approach was that Railtrack had no real idea of the state of those assets.

The whole network was divided into areas, and within each area maintenance was contracted to one INFRACO, replacement of track to another, grinding of rails (when they still were) by yet a different company, delivery of new rails to the trackside by Railtrack itself, to be unloaded by Jarvis or another contractor! This unwieldy system would have defeated even the finest engineering brains – which were not, in any case, employed on the railways.

In theory, these contractors could at least have passed back to Railtrack information about the state of the assets. Sometimes this happened, more often not, and when a contractor was changed in a particular area, such knowledge as had accumulated within a particular firm was generally lost.

Of course, the INFRACOs are not the end of this particular line. As Jimmy Knapp told the Cullen Enquiry, the work was further subcontracted and sub-subcontracted through a bewildering maze of firms. Some of these exist for no purpose other than to supply untrained labour to a railway industry which, like other privatised creations, regarded it as the first test of management virility to reduce the directly employed headcount as far and as fast as possible.

This casual workforce was often unleashed on the network after safety briefings which were sometimes shambolic and occasionally non-existent. Railtrack itself lacked the staff to even begin to monitor the maintenance and renewal process, so the contractors were, in effect, left to get on with it without scrutiny. Bit by bit, the culture of Britain's deplorably unsafe construction sites was imported onto the railways – unsurprisingly, since the same companies were now taking control.[15]

Railtrack's main interest throughout was not, in any case, maximising safety work. How could it be? Every line closure, every speed restriction, meant compensation to be paid by the track monopoly to the train operating companies. 'Safety first' in track maintenance would have come straight out of Railtrack's bottom line, just as train protection systems would largely have come out of the profit margins of the TOCs.

Even given goodwill, such a structure could not be made to work. When one adds in the missing ingredient – that a desire to maximise profit was the only common element, and was often only possible at the expense of some other rail company – it is clear that the whole industry was riding for a fall.

So it was that when the GNER express approached Hatfield on the morning of October 17 2000 the track underneath it shattered into three hundred pieces. One investigator likened it to a 'bicycle crushing a biscuit'. This 'biscuit' did what even the war had failed to do – it brought Britain's railways to a halt.

4

Sweat and Tears on the Tracks

In Margaret Thatcher's view, working on the railways was a sign of personal failure. 'If you were any good, you wouldn't be here,' she was reported to have told BR managers on one occasion.

For the new market-thrust managers who took over the industry upon privatisation, railway workers were a liability to be got rid of as fast as was practical. Before, during and after the privatisation process, senior managers saw it as a test of their mettle to slash the 'head count' of drivers, maintenance workers, middle managers, support and station staff as rapidly as they could. For some, workers with experience of the 'old railway' were the 'enemy within', contaminated beyond redemption through their years of employment in a nationalised public service.

In this respect, if no other, the managers of the John Major railway were true to the anti-trade union attitudes of their Victorian forebears. The Chairman of the South Eastern & Chatham Railway had declared in 1907 that his company would never 'permit a third party to come into their Board Room to discuss with them as to how they are to carry on their business'. The managers of the largest company of all, the London & North-Western, regarded organised labour as a threat to the principles of military discipline on which they sought to found their railway. As in other industries, employers fought the advance of trade unionism every step of the way.[1]

Nor is greed among railway directors entirely a phenomenon of the 1990s and afterwards. Following the first world war, during which the country 'owed a genuine debt of gratitude to all those employed on the railways', in the words of the President of the Board of Trade, this debt was repaid by proposals for a 53 per cent cut in the real wage of railway workers. Those railway directors advancing this plan in the name of industrial competitiveness were simultaneously paying themselves salary increases of up to 150 per cent! Unsurprisingly, they provoked a strike.[2]

Industrial relations on the privately owned railway were forged in the context of such conduct and attitudes. Contrary to contemporary received wisdom, the years of nationalisation were a time of relative industrial peace. In the first twenty years of British Rail, there were only two official national strikes, while disputes after 1965 were generally limited to works-to-rule or one-day stoppages.[3] Many of these, like disputes elsewhere, were related to efforts to maintain real wage rates at a time of high inflation.

Privatisation was introduced, of course, after the position of trade unions throughout Britain had been substantially weakened as an act of government policy. Any reasoned arguments which the unions advanced against privatisation were simply dismissed as the usual special pleading by 'producer interests', although such interests are often in possession of expert knowledge of how to actually run the industry concerned efficiently.

So the new owners of the railway were convinced, by and large, that they both could and should disregard trade unions and dismiss the experience of their staff, and that they should impose acquiescent industrial relations where such did not already exist.

The flaws in this attitude were quickly exposed. Train operating companies were soon in the humiliating position of having to cancel services because they had made too many drivers redundant, notably on South West Trains. And no one could believe that the deteriorating state of the track was completely unconnected with the fact that the workers employed to maintain it were fewer than half the number that they were at privatisation.

The trade unions themselves have had to adapt to the problem of negotiating with up to 100 companies instead of just one, at a time when membership was for some years falling rapidly due to staffing cuts. Yet maintaining the dignity and the conditions of the workforce is an essential part of running an efficient and passenger-oriented railway. When industrial relations break down, as they did with Connex over its aggressive treatment of drivers, or with South West Trains (again) in a dispute over management's attempt to make employees wear bright red waistcoats and name tags, like circus performers, it is the passenger who suffers. Ironically, South West Trains was nevertheless awarded a twenty-year extension of its franchise whilst in the midst of a 'complete breakdown in industrial relations' with its employees, in the words of the RMT union.

The voice of the railway workers has remained largely unheard in the dramas surrounding the industry. But as much as anyone they have borne the brunt of the chaos and crises of the privatised years, not to mention the public anger when the network went into meltdown after Hatfield.

A survey conducted by TSSA, the union which mainly organises white-collar workers in the railway industry, found that fully 81 per cent of members had suffered verbal abuse or insults from passengers in the weeks of chaos following Hatfield. 21 per cent had been threatened with violence and 4 per cent had actually experienced it. More than three-quarters had had to deal with passengers requesting information the staff just did not have.

58 per cent of those surveyed had been asked to take on more work since Hatfield, but 56 per cent felt that their company had been unsupportive.[4] Unsurprisingly, staff morale is rapidly declining. Vernon Hince, Assistant General Secretary of RMT, the largest union for railway workers, told *The Financial Times* that 'morale is low because they [railway employees] can see the service they are trying to provide not being provided.

'In an industry many of them have probably spent 30 to 40 years in, they can see that it's even worse than before or during Beeching', he said, referring to the massive track mileage cut-backs of the 1960s.[5]

The rest of this chapter will tell the story of today's railway in the words of those who work in it, interviewed specially for this book. For obvious reasons, all interviewees were guaranteed anonymity. Their testimony deals not just with industrial relations problems, but also paints a vivid picture of how the railway operates today, under private management, as seen from the inside. None of their words have been added to or embellished in any way.

So we can read here of the signallers told to make passengers miss their connections; of the drivers controlling heavy freight trains for fifteen hours or more; of the guards rung by their 'control' while on duty to check the reasons for a two-minute delay; of the workers not allowed to speak to each other; of the drivers taking 100-mile taxi journeys because the trains are too expensive; of the squabbles as to who will pay for station improvements – and why no one told the signaller about the cow on the line.

Guard, inter-city service

'When trains were running late under BR, connections were held. Now they're not, and things like that which inconvenience the travelling public get taken out on railway staff. The system operates on a penalty basis. If Railtrack causes a delay, it pays the train operator £29 a minute or something like that. But if it is the fault of the train company they pay Railtrack – so they spend all their time writing cheques to each other instead of running a fucking railway. Sometimes I'll be in the train and my 'phone will go and it will be my control ringing, they'll say "you're running two minutes late, what's happening?" and I'll say it's the signals, but they say "Railtrack are telling us it's not them" – this argument is going on over a two-minute delay while the train is still going . . .

'When there was an accident on BR, there was a clear chain of responsibility, which meant there were proper enquiries into incidents and lessons were learnt and applied. If someone was nearly knocked down on the line, for example, there would be an internal enquiry and then a government one. Since Railtrack took over, they just shut up shop. I was once taking a train out and we were going at full tilt, then we got switched onto the wrong line, a bi-directional line going in the wrong direction altogether. So we had a safety meeting, but Railtrack wouldn't hold an enquiry. They said "there's no point, we know what the cause is, water getting into the junction signal box".

In the old days there would have been an in-depth enquiry into how . . .

'Safety suffers from fragmentation. On the track outside this station [a major London terminus] there are three companies responsible, and that's before you even get into sub-contractors. Most of the people with expertise have gone as well. When privatisation came along, they didn't want old railway people, they said "you've got old-fashioned railway ideas". Now you've got people running things who may know about business and finance, but don't know about running a railway. Some of the old BR managers were bastards, but they knew the railway . . .

'What they have done is quadrupled the stress and strain in the job, so the turnover gets higher [a train driver enters the room and adds "they reckon on people leaving after two and a half, three years now"]. Shifts have got longer – we used to have an eight hour day, now it's up to eleven hours, and this is for a safety-critical job. That is what's meant by "efficiency" – fewer people working longer hours. There is just no way at all that this is a better railway now . . .'

Contracts manager, suburban franchise

'My job didn't exist under BR. I have to divide up the cost of the stations my TOC leases from Railtrack. For example [one major station] we manage is used by two or three other TOCs. I then distribute the costs of the station among the TOCs based on how many departures each has each year. It leads to endless arguments – Virgin will say, well, the station only cost so much last year, why is it 10 per cent more now and so on. The whole system is geared up for conflict . . .

'My TOC, like the rest, is a bit of a virtual company. It doesn't own the tracks, it doesn't own the trains, it doesn't own the stations. It's just a name and a few computers, and people like me doing jobs that weren't needed under the old BR when the same company owned the whole lot and there were no contracts. I spend half my time with lawyers now – there's even specialist railway lawyers, which is a new thing. They must have done very well . . .

'It's difficult to say what BR would be like now if it still existed. I hope it would have been a whole lot better because of the enormous traffic growth we've seen. That's been lucky for the private industry, because it's been nothing to do with them. It's been due to economic growth and traffic congestion, they've just reaped the benefits . . .

'The whole thing is so bureaucratic because it's so highly regulated. I'm responsible for our station access contracts, which means that if we want to build a new car park at a station we manage, which is quite common because of more people wanting to use the trains, then I've got to talk to every firm which uses the station as well as Railtrack. Then I draw up a detailed proposal and send it off to the regulator. The woman I deal with at the regulator then wouldn't approve it because they said Railtrack were rooking us, then there was a problem with committing other people to expense beyond the end of our franchise. The document I had to submit had to be in precise wording, then that changed as well. It's now February and this started last July . . . just to build a car park. Under BR it would have been done within weeks, once the decision was made that that's what we wanted to do . . .

'The franchising process is also an inbuilt disincentive to do anything long term. Managers won't look beyond the end of their franchise, at least when it comes to spending money. I don't think the TOCs knew what they were getting into. They're mostly bus companies, really, including mine, and they thought it would be just like running buses, but it's much more complicated. There's limited access to the infrastructure, you have a tightly planned timetable, you get rid of too many drivers, it takes a year to train up some more . . . you can't just take people off the streets. The new managers grossly underestimated the complexity of the task . . . now they're trying to bring back some old railway men to run it.

'I try to be objective, but I really can't see any benefits from privatisation whatsoever. It's no less monopolistic than previously . . . It's not just privatisation, it's the form it took that is so deeply damaging, the fragmentation.'

Train driver, freight company

'Chaos is the only word I can use for it. The railway is now run by crisis management, lurching from crisis to crisis. There is now an epidemic of rest day working, which there never was before. One driver does what should be done by three, there are drivers doing fifty hours a week or even more.

'We used to be on a basic thirty-nine hour week – now it's moved to thirty-seven hours, but it's annualised hours. The problem is the managers just can't manage it. Down at Bescot they're supposed to be on 1,686 hours a year, but one I spoke to the other week had done over 2,000 last year, and I'm going to end up owing about

100 hours which will get written off – it's complete and utter nonsense . . .

'I'll give you an example. Our depot works all the ballast trains on [a main line] over 160 miles down to London. But drivers signing on in London don't get the trains down because the freight companies don't have an arrangement with the TOCs for travel. So they use taxis to get drivers from the depot down to London. Our company's taxi bill last year came to £2 million, and this year it's doubled. And if you over-run, a driver from another company can't relieve you. If a driver from [a passenger operator] was right alongside me he couldn't take over, because his firm ain't going to pay for it . . .

'We're full of safety paperwork, but they don't want to know about fatigue and stress. Fatigue is the main problem . . .

'We used to have seven to nine hours rostering and a pattern of booked work, we could look at our links and what you saw is what you got. Now we have a thing called contract turn, which is the worst thing we've had since privatisation – you never know what you're doing.

'A fifty-five-year-old the other day sent in his letter of resignation. He hadn't even got another job, he just said "I'm fed up to the back teeth." His manger called him in and said "Look, you shouldn't be leaving you should be sticking. What could I do to make you stay?" He said, "Well, I'd want seven to nine hours a day, I want a link that lets me make arrangements for things, and never to do above twelve hours again." The manager said "You know I can't do that." So he's leaving, and this is a guy who's done his whole life in the railway industry. Others are going to passenger companies, or to the new freight companies, which are paying £7,000 more . . .

'When there's a disaster it's poor old passengers, quite rightly, and

I saw one thing after Hatfield saying poor old managers and station staff, but it's never poor old drivers. They only get mentioned if someone's blaming them.

'I would like the government to buy the stake in EWS (English Welsh and Scottish railways) that the Canadians are trying to sell. Why not? Get the investment in freight and in the infrastructure, and get some overall command back. With Railtrack and freight under public control, you would have some unified command.'

Train driver, freight company

'If a passenger company goes bust, the government will have to look after it – in a sense they're still in the public sector. If we go bust, that's it, we're out of a job and forty years' service counts for nowt . . .

'We all work excessive hours. My son's a lorry driver, and he works ten hours a day, but there's no regulations for train drivers. We are working fourteen to fifteen hours and we've had drivers doing over eighteen. There's no way that can be safe. Safety's all talk . . . In our company there used to be one safety rep for each depot, now it's one for each region, so it's gone down from more than forty to six . . .

'Under contract turns they give you a mobile and you can be called in to do any shift, any time at all, with twelve hours notice, and if you haven't got anything you stay at home. So you can be called in to work at any time except when you're on holiday. It's the most detestable thing, you could do five weeks on nights.

'But with privatisation they shot themselves in the foot. Now we can sell our labour to thirty-six different companies, so drivers are leaving EWS ... our depot has lost eight this week. They can go to Virgin, or Midland Mainline, or GNER. I reckon we need another 200–300 drivers to run a proper service, but as soon as they recruit one they lose two. The drivers of what I call pointy-nose trains, the high-speed, they're the cream – GNER, Virgin, Great Western. They get treated more like airline pilots, the others more like bus drivers ...

'I would like to see us go back to nationalisation like it was originally envisaged, but without the bureaucracy and the massive shortfalls of cash. I know we haven't got the money to do it all, because I believe the government should spend money on health and schools first, but if they could just take Railtrack back under public control it would be a start.'

Retired train driver

'British Rail would have done better if it had had the managers the private railways got. They're much better at getting money out of the government than BR was. Only problem is, it doesn't go on safety, it's going to shareholders.'

Driver, inter-city service

'You could call British Rail the "mother railway". It was a massive organisation. It encouraged people to take time off, to get qualifications, there were sporting and social sections. You felt part of a great industry and we felt we were united. Sectorisation was the start of the decline. Decision-making started to be made on business lines, profit centres were creeping in, you started to see the weakening of the trade union . . .

'Fragmenting means drivers just doing inter-city work, just doing local work, whatever, and losing route knowledge. So a train can be sitting in a station going nowhere because there's no driver, even though there could be a man sitting up in the mess room who a year earlier could have driven it, but now he's in the wrong company. At my depot there are now four companies – two passenger, two freight. At one point I could have done any of those routes, and drive all the traction, but now I can only do my own route. Morale started to hit rock bottom in the 1980s and it's not improved since – the mother railway has become a small, privatised company . . .

'[Tory Transport Secretary Cecil] Parkinson said there was an open cheque-book for safety, but the two billion which should have been spent on Automatic Train Protection was spent on privatisation instead. Look at what Railtrack have been doing with track and signalling. In BR days there might have been three to four speed restrictions on my route because of the state of the track, now there are none, and it's not because the track has got better. They have put monitors in stations, and improved facilities, which is welcome, but it's a cosmetic exercise, and they've neglected the track and signalling. On my route there's single track line with Automatic Warning System on it, but it sounds when you pass the signal coming back, from behind, so you think you've passed a red when you haven't. It's a hazard. The HSE isn't happy, drivers aren't happy, our company isn't happy, but Railtrack won't consider changing it. Their arrogance is stunning . . .

'Drivers are always complaining about the track, there's very little replacement. You know when you've hit a rough patch – you can see clay coming up, or water on the clay. Under BR you would have had a speed restriction. Now the pressure is on – work through personal needs breaks, do overtime. They do fourteen to fifteen hour shifts on freight. It must have a long-term physical effect . . .

'Railtrack should be back in public ownership because at the moment they just bully the TOCs. And all the TOCs get this public subsidy which is going into shareholders' pockets, not the industry. British Rail was not perfect. In my time it was all cut, cut, cut; there's more money going in now, but it ends up in people's back pockets. There's enough money to buy it back.'

Driver, inter-city service

'There's a blame culture attached to the driver, but the system almost encourages SPADs. My train was ninety-five minutes late running into London and I got a call about twenty miles out hassling about losing four minutes in the last hour. The pressure's always on – take your personal needs break in the train, travel in the cab with another driver for forty-five minutes, then take over – ten-hour shifts become twelve-, then fifteen-. They're playing on loyalty really . . .

'You're not allowed to deal with anyone else. It's dog-eat-dog . . .

'Management run the railways like they'd run McDonald's. Except for drivers, they take the view that you have to look good, or you're out the door. None of the managers have ever driven a train.'

Driver, regional service

'You can't get work carried out – the TOC says it's Railtrack, they say it's Balfour Beatty, who say it's the subcontractor. You don't know how to get things sorted out . . .

'The TRUST system means you have messages on the cab radio from control about why are you running two minutes late. It's just to sort out who gets the cheque at the end of the day. Railtrack, [driver's company], Virgin all get together once a month and say "you owe me 2,000 minutes", "well, you owe me 1,500", all passing money about the table . . .

'It's embarrassing for drivers when the shit hits the fan. The customer greeters, or whatever they're called, melt away, and it's the train crew and station staff who have to deal with passengers. It's embarrassing when a little old lady asks you when's the next train for London and for twenty years you could say "ten past the hour" and now you haven't a clue . . .

'The gap between drivers has widened now. People move on, follow the money to better-paying operators. My company is just becoming a driver-training school for GNER and Virgin . . .

'The pressure's on, productivity means taking longer and longer shifts, and you see no one else all day long. Say you're on at five in the morning, you leave the house at four, and you're still driving twelve hours later, people wonder why you're yawning. I drive with my cab window open, even in the middle of winter, so the draught can keep me awake. They tell you to beware of "micro-sleep", nodding off for a second. But if you take two minutes at a station to walk along the platform to stay fresh you get TRUST on asking what's happening. Nationalisation's not on the cards, to be honest, but making Railtrack really accountable on safety would be a start. Tighten up on the infrastructure and the trains. I'm driving one which came into service in 1967, but the new ones coming in now, you can see they won't last more than five or ten years.'

Signaller, north-west

'British Rail had many weaknesses, but operating procedures was its strength. There was a clear chain of command, and there was no conflict of interest within the organisation. The operation of the railway came first, and the engineering side was allowed to get on and do its job, it could focus on day-to-day routine maintenance and keeping the system in order. Now the infrastructure is contracted out, they are not working within budgets, but within contracts which they can try to maximise profit out of. If the budget was too low for safety, you could go straight to the board and get it increased. Today, you have to re-negotiate the contract with Railtrack . . .

'If I had problems with equipment in the box, you called out the signalling technician. You still do, but the difference is there's less of them, and a lot of the experienced technicians have gone, so they take much longer coming out and finding the fault, which means that staff are operating the box manually for a longer period now. That's the danger – if you work the box manually for an hour or so, its OK, but if you work it for twelve hours in a busy box, with lots of trains going through there's a danger. It's like if automatic pilot goes off in an aeroplane, for a time the pilot's fine, but then it becomes a real strain.

'When it's on automatic, you have to press just two buttons, one for in and one for out, for each train moving through your patch. On manual, the signaller will press twenty-four, you have to manually set up the route, do a switch for every set of points, and you have no fail-safe except another signaller with you, or a supervisor, who will check your card. If you do that for a whole twelve-hour period, you have a bigger risk of making a mistake, particularly if you have twelve others things to do as well, telephones ringing off the hook . . . all because the technicians now cover bigger areas. BR used to site them where they could get to boxes in the shortest amount of time, now it's all a contract between the infrastructure company and Railtrack. Railtrack is boasting that it has reduced the cost of maintenance drastically. That means less technicians and a contraction of resources. None of it's planned for the requirements of the railway, but for the requirements of the contract . . .

'Railtrack has focused its programme on renewals and station regeneration, not the bread-and-butter stuff of routine, precautionary maintenance, it's not sexy, there's no profits, but it's what keeps the railway running. So they have not replaced wiring, not replaced grease boxes, we're the guys who see it. We get more faults day by day . . . more faults, less fixing . . . apart from the small sections which are being renewed, the network is held together with elastic and string. It's being flogged to death. Some of the junctions the track is in a state of utter disrepair, bouncing up and down. You can see it moving as a train goes through the junction.

'But it's not seen as our role to mention things like that any more. Under BR we would not have had to ring any manager to get something fixed, we would just have rung our local engineering gang and asked them to come and have a look at the junction. Now, I can't call them out. If the track is in shit order, needs lifting and packing, stones putting in, I have to speak to a Railtrack production manager. I can't report it to the engineers, we don't even have the 'phone number of the permanent way gang. They're another company, working to another contract . . .

'We have more paperwork than ever. The bureaucracy is unbelievable. They've buried the job in paper. They're so paranoid about safety that each signal box has a library of books, files, folders, instructions, but it's all just there to cover the backs of the managers. It's so complex the troops don't understand it and haven't got time to read it all. I'm supposed to go to four safety briefings a year. Over the last four years I've attended two altogether, reason being they're so short-staffed on the job and so focused on the budget and penny-pinching that the manager doesn't want me to go off my shift for what he sees as a non-productive day, because they cut back on all relief staff in 1994. They abolished a lot of rest-day relief posts . . .

'A lot of signallers are now working twelve-hour shifts without a break. You have three guys doing eight-hour shifts in a twenty-four-hour box. Say someone wants to go on holiday. There's no relief to cover you, so the only way you can get your day off is if your mates cover and do twelve-hour shifts. Rest day working is a common practice. We're working three Sundays out of four. You're working five basic eight-hour shifts, an eight-hour Sunday shift and an eight-hour rest day every other week. Many work twelve hour shifts, although I won't myself. Work it out . . . it's a fifty-six-hour week before you even talk about twelve hour shifts. There's a culture of overtime. It's cheaper to keep pay low and make 'em work overtime than to pay decent rates and hire and train relief staff.

'The culture of Railtrack is office-based. They don't realise that running trains is the main part of the business. It's all project development and Railtrack property instead. All the people on the operations side, the coalface, are viewed as secondary to contract development and the commercial side. It shows itself in the newsletters – local, zonal, national ones, all dealing with office staff and the big projects. Most of it is irrelevant to signallers. When you're sitting in your box at four in the morning, half your points under two feet of snow, the maintenance crew's not there, trains stuck in the siding and you're trying to get them out, you read in the newsletter that it's some manager's birthday and they're all going for a piss-up at the bowling alley and you're not allowed to drink at all, well, you don't want to know, you don't feel part of a railway any more . . .

'They did a survey last year asking staff what they thought of Railtrack, what we think their priorities are. Funnily enough, they've never released the results. Maybe now, they are coming to terms with the fact that the whole culture needs to change, that they need to put operational people high in the company, but unless it filters through the whole of Railtrack it's worthless. We've heard it all before . . .

'Corbett's last big idea was "empowerment" of staff. We were all to be "empowered", given more responsibility, ending bureaucracy. That was the big message. But because of privatisation and fragmentation we have less power to make decisions than we did under BR. I'll give you an example of what I mean. Under BR, if you were waiting for a connection for the last train home, you wouldn't hesitate to hold the last train on a red light until the main line train had come in, give the passengers a couple of minutes to get across the platform. It's just common sense. That way everyone gets home. Now, in the days of "empowerment", you can't do that. You'd be on a disciplinary charge if you didn't let the last train go on time, at least you would if you did it a few times. It's because you would be costing Railtrack money – it would have to pay the train operator. I got a warning letter from a manager. The manager said the delay cost £350 and I was liable for that. You can't say, well it made sense because the passengers got home and otherwise someone would have had to pay for coaches and taxis to get them home, because Railtrack just say, well, the TOC will have to pay, not us. You can't take common sense decisions any more. You just have to deliver a "train plan", you are responsible for that and you are liable for it. We now have to deliver the plan which delivers maximum profit to Railtrack through access charges and minimises its costs in terms of fines paid to operators. That's the "new railway" for you, and it's not run for the benefit of passengers . . .

'In the box you have a bit of kit, a computer, part of the TRUST system. Every possible delay has a code for it . . . there's a code for "guard in the toilet", a code for "overloading of passengers", code for "points failure". Station X has to input into that computer the code for why each train was late. It's a points system they rely on for sorting out compensation, or there's a row between two controls. I'm spending all my time inputting into the machine causes for delays so they can do their accounts. And I'm always getting calls from the delays controller questioning codes, because they determine who pays who how much.

'There have been instances on a number of occasions when we have been rushed off our feet because the train plan is up the wall, and you're trying to sort it out, keep trains running, 'phones ringing. Well, the first thing I do is switch off TRUST. I'm just not interested, it's not safety critical and I can't sit there inputting data when there's incidents going off to deal with, like I'm giving a train driver authority to pass a signal at danger, and that's the most responsible and crucial thing you can do because then all systems are gone and it's just down to me. But as soon as I've left the computer alone for ten minutes then control come on to me pestering for train times and codes and I tell them to go forth and multiply and put the 'phone down. Then the big boss comes on about the TRUST machine, and I say I'll do it in three hours. They don't like it, but I say "put someone else on the job. Fuck you, you'll have no trains running then." I'd rather face the wrath of a pen pusher than the wrath of a judge or a coroner's court because there's been a crash. That's the real story, every signaller would identify with it.

'Trouble is, younger people in the job are less likely to tell the boss to go and get fucked. Railtrack controllers put pressure on you for commercial reasons. They ask you why a train was delayed for five minutes, you never used to get questioned before, unless a signaller got the rules wrong. You were always told to err on the side of safety, or you'd be justifying yourself to a court. Controllers should not be telling us what to do. Inquiries tell signallers, this is your responsibility, your decision to take, which is a fine thing for enquiry chairmen to say, but they never ask why controllers are then putting pressure on signallers . . .

'Railtrack wanted to get rid of the old British Rail culture, they wanted to get rid of the old railway. They have actually eroded some of the basic instincts of railwaymen. I was trained by an experienced signaller. Now its just flip-chart merchants . . .

'Today on the railways, there's all the divisions – it's control against control. You have Railtrack control, Virgin control, Jarvis control. Now, when drivers 'phone their control, they are not talking to my control. And I'm not allowed to speak to them, in case I tell them something about a delay which goes in their companies' favour. For example, there were cattle on the line in my patch. That can be a major accident if a train hits a cow. The driver should contact me. But he rings his company and tells them about the cattle, they evaluate the situation and get on to Railtrack control, and they evaluate the situation, and by the time Railtrack control tell me, there's been three trains go along the line, travelling at up to 70 miles an hour. Why didn't the driver tell me? He would have done in BR days, but it's all because they are under pressure from their companies to make sure that all possible delays are put down to Railtrack.'

Maintenance worker, south-west

'Our terms and conditions are vastly improved since BR. I don't suppose that was what was meant to happen, but the trade unions have got stronger in some areas. On the down side, there's no job security any more . . .

'Staff shortages are horrific. Even the week after Hatfield, they made a cut of one-third in the maintenance gangs on my area, down from thirty-six workers to twenty-four. It's not the company's fault, though, Railtrack are paying them less so they can't employ the same staff. Railtrack are reducing payments, but the materials cost more, labour costs more, so they can afford to do less and less. The main line now is as bad as the branches . . .

'We are just fire-fighting now, we just respond to problems rather than maintaining. The claim is that the track is walked every week, but really it is just once a fortnight. You walk down on one track and glance over at the other. That is counted as inspecting both tracks, but in my view that is doing it once every other week. The next week you come back and inspect the other track, glancing over at the first one. When I started under BR, all track was checked at least twice a week, and during the day. Now we are doing most of it at night as well, when you can't see half the faults, you can't see the track top. You just can't be sure it's as safe . . .

'If something is urgent, it can still get done right away. But three-day reports [where it is recommended a section of track is examined within three days] never get looked at. You would expect work to be done on three-day reports within seven days, but now it can take up to twelve months. Less serious things never get done until they become urgent. What happened at Hatfield is not uncommon at all, not a bit of it.

'Another difficulty is getting green zones [line closures to allow repair work to be done]. Railtrack just won't give them to us, so a lot of work can't be done. Broken rails are a dilemma for the maintenance company. If you go out on the track and find track faults, my employer could be fined by Railtrack because it slows the trains down and they have to pay the TOCs. People may say "why should I put my employers profits at risk?" Maintenance supervisors are now making decisions on finance like that . . .

'Maintenance staff . . . they pick them up in the bars now, butchers, bakers, builders, people who are all working during the day and then repairing lines at night. The public wouldn't sleep in their beds if they knew what went on. There has been a massive increase in the subcontracting culture. Subcontractors get round the Hidden guidelines [regulating the hours which should be worked on railway maintenance] by only starting the shift when you arrive on the track. I've had someone come down from Motherwell, people from Leeds or Newcastle, and they are not paid for their travel time, so their shift time only counts when they're there, and they're knackered already. It's the maintenance company which picks up the tab, because when you go out and see the mess they've made of the track, they've gone back to Scotland or wherever . . .

'People still do the training, but they don't get the experience working before they're put in charge of jobs. They just pass out of training school, get a certificate and they're doing look-out or taking charge. Used to be in a gang of twelve you'd have eleven experienced and one inexperienced, now the numbers are the exact reverse, only one who'll have the experience . . .

'Rail staff still care about safety, and my company is pretty good – I don't know about the others. There are just too many parties involved. When something went wrong on the old BR, people owned up and said "It was my fault, I'll learn the lesson." Now, no -one owns up, they all say it wasn't down to me, because of all the commercial pressures. So there's no sharing of solutions either . . .

'I'll tell you why there's so many rail breaks – they've laid off all the men who used to pack the joints on the track. Without that, any rail will break. It's not just old rails breaking. And there's a lot more breaks than the figures show. They just call it defective rails or something else, so they don't have to put speed restrictions on. And I haven't seen a rail grinding train in my parts for twenty years at least. We used to have one . . .

'In the same way they call track buckles "misalignments". That's because you have to report track buckles to the HSE, but you don't with misalignments. Faced with a problem, the supervisor calls it something else. You can't blame him. If you have two supervisors on personal contracts, and you have one who puts the passenger first and may stop five or six trains a year and the other takes a chance each time and lets it go, who's going to get the bigger pay rise at the end of the year? The second guy, who takes a chance for the sake of his money may have made the right call, but sooner or later he'll make the wrong one . . .'

Driver, regional railway

'In the first days of privatisation the Managing Director of [my TOC] called me in as the union rep. He was the biggest shyster that I had ever met. He had next to him the former Board Managing Director for regional railways, who was a lovely man. The new MD pointed to him and said "This man will be my eyes and ears." Within twelve weeks he had gone . . .

'My depot used to have drivers from several lines, but it all got rationalised, and now we're all one TOC, which means if another company needs a driver at my station, they can't get one. If the unions had put forward this way of working, we'd have been called Luddites. The owner of the franchise is completely bus-oriented. They know little or nothing about railways. If it wasn't for ASLEF they'd be in a bigger mess than they are anyway – at least we know how to run trains.

'What saved us was this manager we had. He said "Let's get rid of all this sickness. If you get sickness down from 12 per cent to 10 per cent, I'll give you an extra 1 per cent on the pay.' Guys like that made it easier for us to all stand together for our rights through the whole restructuring and privatisation process . . .

'Indifference in this job is fatal. You have to have job satisfaction, you have to feel you are supported by your colleagues and your management. But now we have gross instability. You have drivers doing the same job, you can pay them an extra £1,500 but they can literally just walk across the canteen and get a job with another company because they work a shorter working week or whatever. It has destabilised our grade. Loyalty to the company and the depot is a thing of the past . . .

'The accidents have put the spotlight on management and given them a sense of responsibility. Before that, if you wanted to discuss safety with anyone, you had to make an appointment. It used to be you could just knock on the door and walk in. Now at least the MD says "The buck stops with me" . . .

'It's little things, like dirty trains. Sometimes I can only see out of a bit of the window, the bit the wiper covers, the rest is just filthy. So at the end of every shift, I write in the book "clean windows". And it is just ignored. They say, "we do that every 21,000 miles". That's a lot of journeys if you're on short routes. I said to the manager, "Do you clean your car only every 21,000 miles?" Of course, they got rid of all the cleaners at privatisation. Now all the trains are covered in muck, and that affects passengers as well . . .'

Driver, London suburban franchise

'On my franchise privatisation meant the service collapsed. All the good managers went and were replaced by faceless wonders. There was no dialogue with drivers and no commitment. We lost a lot of experienced managers, that was the start of our problems. The people who were promoted would never have been considered above supervisors' grades before, if that . . .

'The disciplinary culture changed, more Form Ones [disciplinary charges], sickness and attendance became a big issue. It was not the real reason. They said as much – it's not sickness, it's if your face fits. You were dumped out of the industry because some manager had a grudge. Then they started to get rid of people they thought were troublesome, agitating the men and women. And they tried to spread this attitude through ATOC [the Association of Train Operating Companies] – the philosophy to attack and intimidate drivers and other staff. It was an atmosphere of intimidation and fear. They were out to break and harass ASLEF, and they did a great deal of damage to the union's standing with the members . . .

'They threw out the rule book, replaced it with company standards, which they said would make things safer. But drivers were learning from the rule book, and then being tested on company standards, which were completely different . . .

'When the new owners took over there was a distinct lack of traction inspectors. They've increased since, to cope with Railtrack's paper chase, but that's as far as it goes. If you make a comment about safety it goes no further than the company, there's no interface with Railtrack, and there's no desire on the part of them to deal with it anyway. Take speed boards [signs indicating track speed limits]: they used to be nice and clear, now they're cheap plastic ones, always spray-painted and covered with brake dust, so you can't see them . . .

'Since 1986, I have had no update on rulebooks, traction. What I can remember from 1986 is what gets me through my yearly competence exams. We only find out what's in the safety manuals when we come up on a disciplinary charge. Unions have been precluded from any discussions on new procedures. Now there's a paranoia about safety, creating an atmosphere of an accident waiting to happen. We all get training in defensive driving techniques, but that can mean late running, and then you get a bit of paper saying you're on a disciplinary. They say "do defensive driving, but keep to the timetable" . . .

'HMRI [Her Majesty's Railway Inspectorate] are a bloody disgrace. All the years we've tried to have a dialogue with them, but they always change to the company's agenda. Now they're covering their backsides, because they know they could be in the dock along with the Managing Director. British Rail wasn't perfect, but there was a culture of safety. Safety was bred into you as a trainee driver by your fellow drivers. There is now no safety culture bred into anyone in the industry. The drivers, the people working for subcontractors, they care, but the people with financial control are just not interested.'

Safety inspector

'My job is to inspect the safety cases of companies on the railways – making sure they do what they say they are doing, comply with legislation, comply with group standards. We have to do eighty companies, including lots of little set-ups, weed-killing firms, bridge examiners and so on. But we also do the TOCs, the Infracos, the freight companies. We check the competency of drivers and other safety-critical staff. With the ROSCOs we look at the supply chain, the subcontractors, the specialist maintenance, making sure that standards are applied rigorously down the line . . .

'The TOCs have improved; in general safety systems are getting better. But they want us to do unto Railtrack as Railtrack does unto them. We did conduct an audit of Railtrack, but because there was no proper mechanism for agreeing a plan afterwards, and some of the managers disagreed with what was said, nothing was done as a result, even though it predicts almost everything that has happened since . . .

'Railtrack has tried a new approach to asset management, basically "sweating the assets". BR said, for example, that this or that needs renewing every six years. Railtrack said they would look at it, and maybe renew some every four years and some every twenty years. But when they actually examined everything, in 50 per cent of cases renewal was postponed or standards were lowered, so we asked how many things had gone the other way, were being renewed more often. The answer was none at all. It didn't happen. So they were basically sweating the assets, making things last longer. Hatfield came about because of that. The whole attitude is to make things last longer and longer . . .

'Before privatisation there was a big investment hiatus, the state was not investing in the railway. The aim was just to slim down the workforce before privatisation, so as to make it look more attractive to investors. They did not put any maintenance work out, so there were men sitting in depots, looking to do the same work as they did the year before, but they were told, "You've no work to do." Demand was cut falsely, so people were laid off. It was to give the private people a slimmed down workforce. Then they came in and slimmed it down again . . .

'In the industry in general there was a massive exodus of skilled people. Many of them are now consultants, not involved in the railway on a day-to-day basis. The lack of technical staff has become more and more of a problem . . .

'One problem is Railtrack do not want to close the line down to allow work to be done. They do not want to allow possessions. To give an example, a weed-killing firm was hired to cut down trees to stop leaves on the line. Basically they were paid to chop down as many trees on Railtrack land as possible. But because Railtrack would not give them possession of the line, they cut down the trees furthest away from the line in order to meet their targets, where they didn't need possession, and left the ones near the line, which were the ones causing the problem with leaves. It was just so stupid. Railtrack got no benefit from the contract at all . . .

'Another problem we come across is freight trains leaving without the contents of the wagons being properly inputted into the computer. If there was an accident, the emergency services would not necessarily know what is in the wagons. We keep raising it, and the company keep saying "Oh yes, we're going to change", but in the hurry to get the train away, they don't do it. There is just so much pressure on performance . . . Everything is minutes, and minutes cost money. The guys making the decisions, they take chances. They're all on performance-related bonuses . . .

'Now the TOCs are all claiming money off Railtrack post-Hatfield. Where better relationships had been built, this will cause more niggles right down through the organisations, it will be unhelpful.

That sort of thing can impact on safety. It all comes down to fragmentation.'

Platform staff, London terminus

'It's all about flexibility now – that's been the big change. You could be doing shunting one day, and giving out information to the customers on the concourse the next. But there's also lots of things you don't do now because it's all different companies. Carriage cleaning is one company, platform cleaning another, left luggage someone else . . .

'Initial training is adequate, but there's no retraining. They take our guys off the streets, give them a bit of training and that's it for five years. But the bureaucracy's incredible. In our staff room the sink was blocked and the radiator didn't work. For the sink, we had to ring our TOC to get a plumber to come and fix it, but because the radiator counts as part of the building infrastructure, that was Railtrack, so we had to ring them to get another plumber to fix that.

'In the last days of British Rail, when things went wrong, passengers would say to me "Richard Branson's going to sort you lot out, privatisation will sort you out." You certainly don't hear that now.

Booking-office clerk

'Turnover of staff is much higher now. Virgin have a good public image as a brand, so people come to work for it and then find it's not as it's painted, so they get fed up, disillusioned and leave. Used to be you could get free travel across the network, but now it's gone. You only get free travel on your own TOC. It makes it much harder to retain staff in London. Free travel was one of the things that made it possible to do a low-pay, low-skill job in London, but now it's gone . . .

'There's no career progression because of the fragmentation. You can't move on. It's becoming like a McDonald's job, a McDonald's culture, with low wages . . .

'Of course passengers get confused about the fares. A guy says he wants a £10 ticket to Edinburgh and you say, you can't have that, and he'll say, well I could yesterday. No one can keep up with all the ticket offers. They pay a full fare and then get to the other end and see they could have had a special offer, so they then put in for a refund. And then there's trouble because if something's wrong with one route they can't use their ticket on an alternative route, because it's a different company. GNER is particularly bad about that . . .

'We've got a problem with the heating in our building. The TOC says it's up to Railtrack to fix because they own it, Railtrack say it's up to the TOC because we lease it, so it doesn't get fixed and we get freezing cold in the meantime. It's always someone else's problem, no one does anything for themselves . . .

'I think if a private industry goes belly up, it goes belly up. But in this private industry, public money will always stop that happening . . .

Finance manager, inter-city TOC

'Under BR people stayed in the industry for thirty, forty years. Now the turnover is enormous. The first thing my TOC did was carry out huge cut-backs in finance and human resource staff, because we weren't front line, we didn't interface with passengers. Numbers have crept back up since. But the area where numbers have grown massively is contracts. Every part of the railway now has contracts with every other part. We have contracts with other TOCs, with Railtrack, with freight companies, with the old BR property board, with specialist organisations.

'Contracts is the area to be in – you'll never be unemployed in the railway industry if you deal with contracts, that and credit control. A lot of it is still held together because the senior finance people at the TOCs all know each other and used to work together under BR. In ten years time, they'll be gone and God knows how it'll get sorted out. At the moment it is unknown for a TOC to take another TOC to court over an unpaid bill, although there are plenty of them, because the finance guys sort it out . . .

'A lot of the new management has come from outside, and don't have any experience of the railway. They don't understand the unions, or know how to deal with them. My management is petrified of ASLEF, but with TSSA and RMT their attitude is take it or leave it . . .'

Signalling planner, INFRACO

'In the old BR you had the sense of being part of a public service. The relationship between staff and managers was good, and you had job security. The lack of investment was always a problem, on the other hand, and we always seemed to lurch from one reorganisation to another, usually with the purpose of cutting jobs. Lack of investment meant lack of renewals, which affected the state of the track . . . But there was always someone walking up and down the track with the relevant equipment checking, and they were always grinding the rails, which they don't seem to do any more . . .

'Now the people at the top are not railway men, they're construction bosses, and they have a different attitude. Let's face it, construction site safety is not as good as it should be. They have the mentality of cheapest bid, and then cut corners, those sort of attitudes . . . the mentality of the building site, where only a small number of people are on the books, and they bring in agency labour. They don't understand that it can take ten years to get people really good in this business, but they don't listen . . .

'Now they've brought in one hundred skilled workers as designers and testers from India, and other INFRACOs are bringing them in from Romania. Good as they are, their first language isn't English and out on the track, well think of the safety implications. They're paying Indian Railways £33,000 per year per man for them; what happens to the money after that I don't know . . .

'[My INFRACO] are not very good in how they treat people. They treat us like crap, which you never had under BR. Safety is not all that it might be. It's not so much penny-pinching as a lax attitude.

People are very over-tired at our company. They're very funny about people taking rests after weekend work, people have to fiddle the time sheet to get a break because the chap in charge says "I'm not paying people to rest." That can't go on – people are pushing themselves too far . . .

'Most of us just stay in the industry now for the travel facilities and the pension. On the old railway your *raison d'être* was looking after the public to the best of your ability, but [the INFRACO] does not want us to do that. They believe people work best when they're frightened. You can imagine how that goes down on the track. Our manager insists on sacking a couple of people every week to help keep people on their toes. It leads to stress and depression, to that feeling that you lack control, that no one's interested in what you have to say. Most people are quite ill, but they soldier on. Ruling by fear is terrible, but that's all construction bosses know. If you do the job under time, you get a bonus, if you do it over time, you're doing it on your own time. So of course, people run risks to get a job done on time. It's a poisonous atmosphere . . .

Signaller, East Midlands

'When I started in 1980 it was a close-knit family. Everybody was under the same umbrella – signallers, station staff, guards, drivers at the depot, all under the area manager who was part of the Division. Then they did away with the Divisions, and the area manager had to stand alone, and that lasted four or five years and then we became a profit centre or business centre. We were all split up – provincial railways, inter-city, trainload freight, and then that was split up again into different sectors, trainload freight petroleum, trainload freight parcels and so on. Everything was done through the profit centre . . .

'Railtrack sees the operation of the railway as a bit of a hindrance to its role, which is more being a substantial property company. The management structure of Railtrack is bloody abysmal. I used to criticise the old management set-up but I have never seen anything like it. They snow everybody under with paperwork, but no one actually does anything unless something goes wrong, like Hatfield, when they get caught out . . .

'Now I can get told to put a freight through in front of an express because it's a way of avoiding penalty payments. The pressure in the major power boxes is completely different – you've got regulators, delay attribution clerks and you're forever on the 'phone so someone can blame someone else, so Railtrack can say "It's not us Guv, it's your driver." Anything apart from come clean. It's crap . . .

'Now everybody is scrutinised. They tell you it's to improve performance, minimise delays. We get faxes every day about the performance of your area with smiley faces on it if you've done well and glum faces if you've caused so many minutes' delay. So Doncaster is smiley faced, because it's done fine. It's a load of bollocks. If you don't meet performance targets you get a letter saying "This is costing us money, it's imperative to Railtrack's very survival" . . .

'You join the railway thinking it's a public service but now it's business-oriented, profit-oriented. Many, many different fragments making money and all competing against each other. On my telephone in the box there's a sticker saying "Who is it? Why are they calling? Should we tell them?" If you turn the clock back, there was a central control, everyone knew why a driver was delayed if he was. Now every company has its own control, and everyone tells them before they tell Railtrack. If a train fails, I need to know in the signal box instantly, but the driver 'phones his own company and maybe they tell me ten minutes later. They just think, let's wait and see what happens . . .

'You used to see the track being walked every day, but you hardly ever see anybody now. And the rulebook has been changed dramatically. It used to be that when the work had to be done, the line was blocked and that was that. Now a lot of the permanent way gangs have been cut and there are not enough men to do the job properly, as it should be done and as it used to be done. Corners get cut. They are taking possession with no look-out, or no intermediate look-out on high speed lines. It's a miracle that worse hasn't happened . . .

'Little has changed since Hatfield. We were told it was all going to be done differently. They [management] panicked. You can't tell me they didn't know of all those faults – defective rails, gauge-corner cracking – years ago . . .

'One of two things are inevitable unless Railtrack mends its ways. Either it will go completely bankrupt because it will not have the finances to do the work that needs to be done, or the government will take it over. Railtrack cannot possibly meet the financial burden or make the profits required . . .

'The railway will always be no bloody good unless there are railwaymen in charge of it. What did Gerald Corbett ever know about the railway? Sweet FA. You can't compare the railway with anything else, not ICI, British Coal, Woolworths or whatever.'

5

Sorry Is Not Enough

Hatfield was the crash which became a crisis. The derailment last October led to the greatest disruption which the world's first railway network has seen in its 160-year history.

Within a day of the disaster, Railtrack had admitted that the cause of the accident was almost certain to be the state of the track in the area. This cannot have come as a shock to the track monopoly, as it was clearly advised about the deteriorating state of the line near Hatfield almost a year previously.

Yet the crash galvanised Railtrack. It leapt from passivity to panic in a single bound. A network which it had regarded as wholly safe just a week earlier was suddenly found to be in such urgent and comprehensive need of repair as to require almost total shut-down. Within hours the northern part of the West Coast mainline from London to Glasgow was completely closed, leaving travellers stranded. Hundreds of speed restrictions were imposed throughout the network in a matter of days, leaving timetables in ruins and passengers and train operators in the dark.

Clearly, this was not the result of a comprehensive overnight inspection of more than eleven thousand miles of track, bringing to light hitherto unsuspected weaknesses. There was insufficient time for that. Railtrack can only have been acting on information about the state of the infrastructure which it already largely had in its possession, but had, pre-Hatfield, regarded as being safe to ignore (or too costly to acknowledge).

Indeed, the mass line closures and speed restrictions may well not have been an engineering decision at all. It would have been slightly unusual if it had been, since Railtrack is an organisation as light on senior engineers as it is heavy on accountants and lawyers. It was probably its legal team which ordered the shut-down of Britain's railway network.

'Exporting the risk'

One man who certainly thought so was Strategic Rail Authority boss Alistair Morton. He accused Railtrack lawyers of telling management to 'export the risk' by virtually closing the network down, thereby ensuring that if anything else went wrong, it would be somebody else's fault. It was Railtrack's way of saying that since it could not run the railway safely, it would not run it at all and that way nobody would get hurt. Sir Alistair said:

The fear that our system has a cancer in its innards joined up with a realisation that our boffins did not fully understand a metallurgical problem affecting a truly primary component of the rail system – the rails. The reaction was that Railtrack, supported by the HSE, exported the risk to everyone else by speed restrictions . . . Railtrack was impelled to do this (by) lawyers and advisers.

This left the operators struggling to contain the risk that had been poured from the Railtrack bottle. The fact that they have not been supremely efficient in coping with that unexpected transfer of widely disseminated risk is not entirely surprising . . .

Elsewhere Morton said that Railtrack 'have exported risk to everyone else. By doing that they have caused maximum inconvenience to everyone else.'[1]

The same point was made by the Chairman of the Rail Passengers Council, Stewart Francis. He told a conference that 'in the last few weeks we have effectively seen Railtrack saying "OK – you all want a safe railway and we do not want to expose ourselves to threat. So we will hobble the network with speed restrictions until we are convinced that our exposure has been limited." This would not have happened under BR.'[2]

In other words, protecting profit, not protecting lives, was at the bottom of Railtrack's apparently ill-considered response to Hatfield. Indeed, the sudden slapping on of hundreds of new speed restrictions may actually have increased, rather than reduced, the risk to passengers.

An internal and unpublished Railtrack report warned that these new restrictions could increase the risk of a driver passing a signal at danger, because of the confusion and the need to absorb masses of fresh pages of driving instructions relating to the multitude of new speed restrictions. Certainly, the increased overcrowding on both trains and stations caused by the chaos was an additional risk, while the fact that passengers and freight were displaced onto far more dangerous roads could only cost additional lives. In reality, Railtrack's legal-led 'safety first' strategy was its exact opposite.

Shutting down the network was only one part of Railtrack's immediate response to Hatfield. If the first prong of its strategy was dictated by lawyers, the second was targeted at what had become the company's key constituency, the City institutions. The Railtrack board voted to *increase* its dividend payment to shareholders. Apparently oblivious to the chaos around them, directors felt that now was the time to raise the interim dividend by 5 per cent to 9.75p per share. Chief Executive Gerald Corbett said the increase was a signal to shareholders that better times were ahead. Even in an era inured to the excesses of corporate greed and irresponsibility, this seemed like a gratuitous insult to the public, for whom better times on the trains seemed so far ahead as to be invisible.

Mick Rix, leader of the train drivers' union ASLEF probably spoke for that public when he said that it was 'extraordinary that the Railtrack board, while presiding over a shambles unprecedented in the railway industry, should feel that this is the moment to increase rewards to shareholders rather than putting extra money into maintenance and other investment.'

In an unusual display of cross-industry harmony, the same view was expressed by the chief executive of Sea Containers (owner of the GNER franchise) a few months later. James Sherwood observed drily: 'Railtrack, in a series of rather baffling moves, first increased its dividend pay-out to shareholders, then said it needed more subsidy from the government . . .'

The dividend increase was, however, the parting signal from Corbett. The Railtrack board asked him to quit the same week. It was generally assumed that he was paying the price for Railtrack's unenviable safety performance, though it seems more likely that he was actually carrying the can for Railtrack's reaction to the Hatfield crash, rather than its responsibility for the tragedy. 'Zero tolerance' of track problems may have made good sense to the company's lawyers but it was, as one trade publication put it 'politically unsustainable for the government, practically impossible for the rail traveller and last, but by no means least, financially crippling for train operators. All in all, it was a policy decision too far.'

Railtrack in the dock

Corbett was replaced by a duo of managers who could claim just thirteen months' experience in the railway industry between them. New Chief Executive Steven Marshall had joined Railtrack from the drinks industry a year earlier, while new Chief Operating Officer Jonson Cox had arrived from Yorkshire Water just six weeks before Hatfield.[3]

They took over a company which had, finally, used up its stock of public patience. The Chief Inspector of Railways, Vic Coleman, the man ultimately responsible for safety in the industry, announced that he considered the privatisation of Railtrack a grave mistake which had contributed to safety problems, an unusually blunt statement from a public servant.

The Rail Passengers Committee for Southern England said that public confidence in the railways was at 'probably its lowest point ever.' Chairman Wendy Toms noted: 'If astronomers using computers can track the progress of black holes in galaxies trillions upon trillions of light years away, it should be possible for Railtrack to monitor the pattern of faults on its railway lines.'[4]

The industry's regulators also queued up to blame the track monopoly. Sir Alistair Morton of the SRA said that

Railtrack is a private sector company in the painful process of understanding, perhaps for the first time, that it has a public service obligation. Railtrack is having to recognise something that Gerald Corbett was unable to recognise, that Railtrack is only able to make money out of fulfilling a public service obligation. Railtrack should be a public service deliverer . . . Railtrack has to find a new chairman who understands that, and a board who understands that. Railtrack has not been accustomed to that notion.

And Rail Regulator Tom Winsor told a committee of MPs that 'Railtrack, for too long, believed it . . . was a dictator to the industry and the train operators must come to Railtrack as supplicants . . . It must become far more customer-focused and customer-oriented than it ever was before, and I believe that under the old regime it didn't understand that.' These words were, of course, deeply ironic, since it was in the name of customer service that the Tories had embarked on the whole privatisation of the industry and the creation of Railtrack in the first place.[5]

Railtrack was the proverbial sitting duck. It was the core of an industry suffering a public and prolonged meltdown. Yet the behaviour of the other main actors in the privatised industry left none in line for customer care awards.

Widening margins

The infrastructure and maintenance companies, for example, saw opportunity where others saw tragedy. The state of the track revealed at Hatfield would surely help their case for more money and less pressure from Railtrack, they calculated. Not everyone took their special pleading at face value. Sir Alistair Morton had been thinking of the maintenance system above all when he referred to a 'cancer' in the railway.

Trade magazine *Modern Railways* reported in the midst of the crisis that 'the maintenance contractors will see Hatfield as the opportunity to widen their margins.' Interviewing Morton, the magazine accused Railtrack of 'treating contractors like rogues and screwing prices down', to which the SRA boss simply replied: 'Contractors are rogues.' His Chief Executive, Mike Grant, warned in the course of the same interview that 'we have to protect ourselves against [being] taken advantage of on a commercial basis, as a result of the crisis.' Clearly men who knew who they are dealing with.[6]

Nor did the train operating companies exactly rise to the challenge, despite the efforts of many front-line staff. As the network ground to a standstill, any notion of customer service seemed as far from their minds as it was from Railtrack's. The TOCs failed to supply accurate and timely travel information to frustrated passengers. Their own operational failings – like rolling stock breakdown – added to the misery. There were no reports of any franchise holder risking its finances by hiring additional station staff to help cope with the crisis, for example.

In fact, the train operators responded in the way that might have been expected by any student of the privatised industry. First, they reached for their lawyers, deluging Railtrack with compensation claims. This, of course, was inherent in the fines-and-contracts cement which binds the industry together. The TOCs initially claimed £300 million for lost track access, and have been working their way up from there.

Second, the train operators proved that, whatever else Railtrack has a monopoly of, it does not include crass insensitivity. At the turn of the year many TOCs announced fare rises to impose on those passengers heroic enough to be still attempting to make journeys by train. Those fares which are not regulated were raised by up to 4.9 per cent, well in advance of the rate of inflation. The biggest increases were announced by franchises run by National Express Group, the largest of the new rail monopolies, with some of the lowest customer satisfaction ratings. Stewart Francis of the Rail Passengers Council described this as 'a kick in the teeth for passengers'. Gwyneth Dunwoody, the formidable Labour chair of the Commons Select Committee on Transport, called the increases 'barmy' and short-sighted.

The increases consolidated Britain's unenviable position of having the highest standard rail fares in the world. The situation is, to no one's surprise, worse where a private monopoly is tightest. London to Manchester fares, entirely in the grip of Virgin Trains, have risen by 50 per cent in the last two years.

At this point, the man with ultimate responsibility (if not power) over the whole industry, Deputy Prime Minister John Prescott, waded in. 'I have asked the rail authority,' he announced, 'to give me a full report on it. I know it has caused a great deal of concern.' What Mr Prescott did not seem to know, however, was that there was nothing he could do about the increases, since, as the Chairman of the Association of Train Operating Companies George Muir pointed out to him, 'rises for unregulated fares are a commercial decision for each train operating company – the vast majority are demand-driven.'[7]

When it made the requested report, the Strategic Rail Authority told the deputy prime minister the same thing – that it was none of his business. In expressing the frustration of passengers with an arrogant and greedy industry, Prescott also unwittingly drew attention to his own and the public's impotence in the context of a privatised industry. The lobbying group Transport 2000 pointed out that 'in blaming the companies for increasing fares the government is "privatising the blame" when it's the government's responsibility for determining fares regulation – a responsibility it has so far shirked.'

Indeed, *The Financial Times* observed that that the fares episode 'is another embarrassment to Mr Prescott, who has been criticised for making bullish promises that could not be upheld,' words which could be an epitaph on the government's entire stewardship of the rail industry.[8]

Even when a TOC made a dramatic consumer-friendly gesture, it seemed to backfire. Virgin, for example, announced half-price tickets to all destinations for the month of February 2001 in a bid to woo passengers back to the trains. They rather spoiled the effect, however, by boasting that they had kept the move secret from all the other train operators when it was clear that what the public were crying out for was a co-ordinated response to the loss of passengers from all parts of the fragmented industry.

The shine was still further taken off the initiative when, just a month after the end of the cut-price offer, Virgin announced a 10 per cent increase in fares on its main routes, blaming the move on a post-Hatfield profits slump. The alternative, the company said, was to 'hand back the keys' to the franchise, a development which many passengers would heartily welcome, even if the threat chilled the bones of ministers.

Companies in trouble

Virgin was not alone in feeling the squeeze. The ubiquitous Sir Alistair Morton – who every day seemed to denounce the conduct of another fragment of the industry, for all the world as if he was not supposed to be in charge of it – accused the train operators of 'covering their backs' during the crisis. They were not covering their costs, however. The post-Hatfield crisis pushed several TOCs towards the point of insolvency. It was estimated that the TOCs lost 19 per cent of their revenue (£163 million) between Hatfield and the turn of the year.

As described above, the great majority of passenger franchises are held by much larger transport conglomerates, able to cover any rail-related losses for a time and wait for the compensation cheques to roll in from Railtrack and the subsidy cheques to roll in from government. Those franchises without a corporate sugar daddy were, however, soon in trouble.

GB Railways, operator of the Anglia franchise in the eastern counties of England, was the first to push the panic button. A consortium created solely for the purpose of bidding for rail franchises, it lacked the deep pockets of a Stagecoach or a National Express. Anglia's income fell by a third in the aftermath of Hatfield,

leading the government to put a team of SRA executives on stand-by
to take over the operation should it collapse. In the end, Railtrack
expedited Anglia's compensation claim, sparing the government what
would have amounted to a *de facto* renationalisation of a rail
franchise. Other franchises reported to be suffering particular difficulties included GNER, Virgin, Midland Mainline and ScotRail.
Overall train operator profits were down by 7.3 per cent, according
to figures published in March 2001, with regional franchises doing
worst and London commuter franchises the best.[9]

The position of freight companies was, however, worst of all.
Post-Hatfield the largest operator, English Welsh and Scottish railways, was cancelling anything up to 400 trains a week and running
most of the remainder late. With its US parent Wisconsin Central
already up for sale and with potential purchasers looking askance at
the British operation, this could not have come at a worse time for
the company. Freightliner, the second largest company in the sector,
was estimated to be losing £1.1 million per month because of the
crisis. 'Obviously, we're more than upset. Over the past four-and-a-
half years we have built this business up by 40 per cent. That's in
jeopardy,' the company's managing director said.[10]

Moving freight off roads on to rail had been an article of faith (at
least rhetorically) for the Labour government – indeed, even its Tory
predecessor had paid lip-service to the concept. Environmental arguments and the clear economic benefits of diminished road congestion
all indicated the desirability of a reversal of the fifty-year shift of
freight haulage from rail to road. Indeed, prior to Hatfield, rail
freight had been growing considerably. This, however, mainly
reflected a rebound from the artificially depressed levels created by
the slash-and-burn approach to freight followed by British Rail top

management in the company's last years, with custom being driven away by huge price increases. Railtrack was already under fire pre-Hatfield within the industry for its perceived indifference to freight customers – the company saw little commercial advantage in securing greater usage by freight trains, and its exorbitant access charges reflected that policy. Government, too, was ambivalent, agreeing in 2001 to allow access to Britain's roads for much larger continental lorries, against the recommendations of its own Commission on Integrated Transport – testimony to the overweening power of the road lobby even in the face of original government intentions.

So the rail freight industry was ill-prepared for the further blows it would sustain as a result of the crisis on the network. The position of freight operating companies (FOCs) was different, and worse than that of their TOC cousins in two respects. Firstly, the passenger side of the industry could, no doubt, hope that passengers would eventually return once the crisis had passed, for want of a viable alternative way of moving around if for no other reason. However, the whole history of rail freight shows it is far, far harder to win back customers once lost. Once a firm has made the decision to invest in road haulage instead – purchasing lorries and setting up road depots, or negotiating a contract with a haulage firm – it is unlikely to reverse the decision and go back to rail without the most compelling economic inducements. A transport manager with a fleet of lorries stuck in traffic jams would nevertheless feel more in control and less helpless than one with goods parked in a rail siding waiting on the mercies of the impenetrable control centres of the fragmented railway.

Secondly, if a passenger franchise were to go belly up, the government, via the SRA, would ultimately have to step in and run the operation until it was refranchised to a new company. There is no such safety-net for FOCs – the SRA merely has an option, rather than an obligation, to step in. Should they go bust then, in principle, at least, that is that, and it is no more the government's concern than if a chain of supermarkets, for example, went into liquidation. Whether in practice any government could actually sit there with arms folded while millions of tonnes of freight went back onto the roads, blasting a hole in economic and environmental policy as it did so, remains to be seen. But clearly the threshold for government intervention and assistance is very much higher for a freight operator than for a passenger franchise, the more so given the unremitting pressure from the powerful roads lobby to have policy and resources tilted in its direction.

Passenger misery

However, it was the misery of the passengers which, not surprisingly, attracted the most attention. As the chaos mounted, you could take your pick of the travellers' tales which started filling the newspapers:

— A Midland Mainline service from London to Nottingham took nine hours rather than the usual one hour forty-five minutes. A power failure led to a four-hour delay, followed by the closure of the line north of Kettering because of maintenance work. Buses finally got weary passengers to Nottingham in, as one report pointed out, 'the time it would take to fly from London to Bombay'.
— Passengers arriving at Stansted airport on Boxing Day found that

the last train from the airport to London had left before the last seven scheduled flights in had even landed. The last coach had gone, too – both run by the transport monopoly National Express. NEG's desire to save on overtime payments meant that airport staff had to scurry around to hire extra coaches and taxis to get passengers into London, many had to wait hours before they could leave the airport.

— A trip from Blackpool to Halifax, a distance of 75 miles, on Northern Spirit, took ten hours rather than the scheduled one hour and three-quarters. This nightmare journey included many of the usual features – substitute bus services, non-existent trains at Preston – with one unusual addition: when a train finally left Preston for Halifax, it got no further than Accrington, just a few miles down the line, before turning round and heading back to Preston again.

— A Virgin train from Newcastle arrived in Plymouth sixteen hours after departure – delays included cancelled connections and a four-hour wait on the motorway because a replacement bus suffered a puncture!

— A journey from Edinburgh to Southampton took sixteen hours after, in the words of one trade journal, 'a series of mishaps including track failure, power failure and eventually engine failure'.[11]

Not all of these delays were due to Railtrack's 'recovery programme'. Weather played a part, as did defective rolling stock and incompetent management at the TOCs. But the distinctions were understandably lost on passengers, who saw nothing but a railway in chaos, as incapable of informing them as to what was going on as it was unable to run an efficient service.

The overall effect on the economy also became severe. On a conservative estimate, the disruption was costing the nation at least £6 million each day, with some regions particularly hard hit as a combination of rail chaos and weather left major cities virtually isolated from the wider world. Road congestion, which is estimated by National Economic Research Associates to cost about 1 per cent of the country's gross domestic product, was made still worse.

The London Chamber of Commerce estimated that thirty million working hours and £600 million were lost in the capital in the last quarter of 2000 because of the rail crisis, and that losses for the country as a whole could be five times higher. A survey of the finance directors of Britain's top 250 companies found that 42 per cent believed productivity had suffered as a direct result of rail disruption, while 92 per cent believed it had tarnished the overall image of British industry.[12]

'Recovery programme'

This growing alarm finally penetrated Number 10 Downing Street, where railways had been dismissed as 'not a priority' in the early months of Tony Blair's administration. Leaders of the fractious industry were summoned to weekly head-banging sessions at Downing Street by an exasperated premier as autumn turned to winter and the number of speed restrictions on the network stayed stubbornly high. Trade Unions, however, were not invited.

Little seemed to change as a result of prime ministerial intervention. Perhaps this was when it first began to be dimly understood within the political and economic elite that there might not actually be any possible solution within the framework and structure of the industry as it was constituted. Certainly, Railtrack and TOCs alike seemed determined to leave everyone with no alternative to that conclusion as the 'recovery programme' degenerated into farce.

It swiftly became clear that, having all but closed down the network, Railtrack lacked the management and engineering resources to put its 'possession' to good effect. The numbers of people hurled into the breach to carry out repairs every weekend sounded impressive, until it is became clear that many had not a clue what they were doing, and that Railtrack was denuded of managers with sufficient railway experience to oversee them.

Some staff brought in to address the crisis were left standing idle for days awaiting equipment, instructions or both. One employee told *The Observer* that 'I've spent most of the last week sitting in a wagon drinking tea . . . the chain of command is as long as this bloody track', while another said that 'everyone wants to pull out the stops and get this done, but the management structure is pulling the opposite way. People would be scandalised to know how much time is being wasted.'[13]

Undoubtedly, in the crisis after Hatfield, the country paid the price for the industry's years of job-cutting. Two rounds of redundancies, first by British Rail as it was slimmed down for privatisation and then by the INFRACOs and Railtrack itself in order to maximise profits, had left it without the human wherewithal to cope. To take just one small example from the East Coast Main Line, the two track maintenance managers had been earlier reduced to one. Why? *Modern Railways*' conclusion that it was because 'Railtrack saw itself reflected in the City's mirror as a money machine, and believed that the railway would engineer and run itself as it had always done' seems inescapable.

A House of Commons committee reporting on the industry chaos arrived at the same view:

> Although Railtrack's decision to place a greater priority on engineering is welcome . . . it suggests that the company had previously lost sight of the fact that its core responsibility is to run a safe and efficient railway, and that to do so requires Directors and management with appropriate experience and knowledge . . . Railtrack should look again at its senior management and appoint to its Board and to other senior positions people with knowledge and experience appropriate for running the railway.

One contractor, AEA Technology Rail, has admitted that it is short of skilled workers in nearly every employment area, while another, First Engineering, has claimed that responses to job advertisements are insufficient to meet demand. The Rail Industry Training Council has admitted that the problem is 'grave'. This national skills shortage not only hampered the 'recovery programme' after Hatfield, but also threatens to create a bottleneck on the delivery of ambitious investment plans for the future.[14]

Railtrack's response to Hatfield did include the appointment, for the first time in the company's history, of a chief engineer to oversee maintenance, and the offering of £1,000 bonuses to graduates by way of a 'golden hello' if they joined the beleaguered company. More in keeping with its corporate tradition, it also advertised for an external engineering consultancy to take over the job of monitoring and checking on work, at a contract said to be worth £450 million over nine years. Perhaps the consultant could yet turn out to be one of the INFRACOs, which would thereby end up checking their own work – or would yet another firm be added to the retinue of contractors and subcontractors crawling over the assets of the fragmented railway?[15]

The deadline for restoring the network to 'normal' operation continually slipped throughout the winter, in what is close to becoming a British tradition in relation to the completion of major engineering projects – first it was Christmas 2000, then Easter, then the summer, then the end of 2001, then beyond . . .

All the while, to add insult to injury, it was revealed that £700 million worth of new trains were marooned out of service because of what were described as 'technical or bureaucratic hitches' in certifying them fit to use. Such is the shortage of testing facilities, for example, that British-built trains have had to be taken abroad to be tested before being returned for use on British tracks. Another hold-up has been the difficulty manufacturers have had in making the trains operationally compatible with Railtrack's electrical signalling systems. This has been attributed to Railtrack's failure to release full details of the system. One industry observer was quoted as observing that 'the level of collaboration between Railtrack and the manufacturers is not as good as it should be' which is, naturally, par for the privatised course. In the meantime those passengers lucky enough to get a train on many franchises were likely to be getting into old, dirty or unsafe slam-door rolling stock while gleaming new trains remained stuck in the sidings.[16]

A microcosm of the mayhem, the modernisation of Leeds station also stands as a monument to Railtrack's mismanagement. This work had nothing directly to do with the post-Hatfield track renewal programme. It was, in fact, the first (and, so far, only) part of the long awaited upgrade of the East Coast Main Line from London to Leeds and Edinburgh – a project to increase the number of lines out of the station's western end. This was a large, but not especially complicated project of the sort which railway engineering companies have undertaken as a matter of routine down the years.

Railtrack's original schedule called for the station to be shut down over the Christmas period to allow the resignalling and laying of new tracks to be undertaken uninterrupted. As it was, completion of the project was repeatedly delayed, leaving those wishing to visit or leave England's third largest city by train marooned. January 2 slipped to January 4, then to January 8, and then to an incomplete reopening on January 15. It remains unclear whether the work actually took far longer than it should, or whether Railtrack's original estimate for completion was simply another symptom of its corporate ignorance as to the basics of railway engineering.

Certainly, it was boom time for Yorkshire coach companies, as passengers arriving at Leeds station were herded onto road transport to the nearest open railway stations, and for shops in nearby York-shire towns, which enjoyed extra Christmas trade because shoppers could not make their usual journey into Leeds. As late as Easter, services from the station were still chaotic. It all symbolised a system overwhelmed by fairly straightforward tasks. Coming in the midst of a patent inability to cope with a crisis as well, it added to the sense of an industry out of control.

Similar problems afflicted Christmas engineering work at the huge railway yards at Willesden, north-west London. Again, these were long-planned improvements which formed part of the massive (and massively delayed and over-budget) modernisation of the West Coast route. Come the New Year, only local services were able to operate into and out of Euston, London's busiest inter-city terminus, as a result. This provoked the usual name-calling and finger-pointing. One train operator was quoted as complaining that 'Every day over the Christmas period, there's been a cock-up ... Railtrack just cannot deliver its promises.'

Another affected to be shocked by the dawning belief that 'Railtrack is behaving like an organisation which owes its allegiance to the City and the shareholders' rather than the public interest.' An accurate observation – but there must be a suspicion that the same is true of the train operating company employing the anonymous complainant.[17]

Regulators and government

This picture would, in all conscience, have been chaos enough for a completely unregulated industry. For one with enough regulators to start a barber-shop quartet, could they only sing from the same sheet, the mayhem seemed all the more inexcusable. Where were the regulators – DETR, SRA, HMRI and ORR to give them their full initials – in the industry's hour of need? At each other's throats, like the industry itself.

The Strategic Rail Authority's Alistair Morton had certainly been free with his opinions concerning every other player. Indeed, his behaviour recalled the executive style of Baroness Thatcher who was reported, during her administration, to be forever in a state of exasperation with the conduct of government as if it had had nothing to do with her. Sir Alistair is, indeed, a prototype businessman of the Thatcher era. A tough manager with an abrasive reputation in industrial relations earned while in charge of the construction of the Channel Tunnel, Sir Alistair brought to his responsibilities an unswerving commitment to the virtues of private enterprise and a disdain for political interference in business.

However, even this Genghis Khan of capitalism appeared confounded by the problems of the 100 piece railway. One very senior industry executive was privately contemptuous of Morton and the SRA in the author's presence: 'He has no credibility in the industry whatsoever. It's all very well running around making after-dinner speeches if you have the staff underneath you doing the serious, quality work. He hasn't. The SRA is a dead duck.' The joke that the SRA had neither strategy nor authority developed rapidly into the accepted wisdom throughout the industry. Few can be found to disagree with the judgement of *The Times*: 'The SRA . . . has so far proved a disappointment: uncertain in its role, unable to think strategically and without proper resources.'[18]

The SRA's case was not helped by repeated delays in producing its strategic plans and similar endless hold-ups even in its bread-and-butter role of letting and re-letting passenger franchises. Although the much-despised Connex was removed from the London and suburban South Central franchise (in favour of Go Via, itself a firm with a chequered record) the equally controversial Stagecoach was given a new twenty-year franchise for South West Trains. This in spite of a record of running dirty, late and overcrowded trains for years on one of the busiest London suburban routes.

That renewal, re-letting the Chiltern franchise to the incumbent, and announcing a huge increase in the subsidy to be paid to Arriva for operating the Northern Spirit franchise, was the full extent of the SRA's activity on the franchising front as of the spring of 2001.

And even the little it was doing increasingly fell foul of Railtrack. The Chiltern deal has not been finalised because Railtrack could no longer commit itself to £150 million of improvement work on the line. Likewise, a two-year extension of the Midland Mainline franchise was stymied when Railtrack backed away from commitments to track upgrades and new stations. With bidding for the Central Trains franchise in the midlands halted by the SRA because of the poor value of the bids made, the franchising process seems to be going nowhere.

The SRA's authority problem was highlighted when it confronted Railtrack over the future of the mangled East Coast Main Line. It was a dispute which highlighted the fundamental impossibility of making a workable silk purse out of the sow's ear of privatisation.

In a nutshell, Railtrack announced that the cost of its upgrade of the line, which got off to such a stumbling start at Leeds station, was likely to be considerably more than the £2 billion (perhaps as much as £4 billion) previously announced. The SRA thereupon announced that it was suspending the refranchising process, a contest that had pitted the incumbent GNER (a subsidiary of Sea Containers) against Richard Branson's Virgin Trains, run in partnership with Stagecoach.

Submissions from the two bidders had outlined different requirements for the line, with the Virgin plan including substantial stretches of entirely new high-speed track. Faced with this suspension of the franchising process, Railtrack then completed the catch-22 scenario by declaring that it would not go any further with the upgrade work until the future train operator was clarified and Sir Alistair had produced his strategic plan for the line.

This perfect picture of paralysis was only broken when the SRA agreed to back down and accept Railtrack's new cost estimates before ruling that the whole upgrade should be placed in the hands of a 'joint venture' of unspecified partners. And that may not be the end of the ECML row. Richard Branson, already the jilted suitor of the national lottery, has threatened to take the whole controversy to court if the SRA denies him his objective, which is to establish a Virgin monopoly on trains from London to Scotland. And Morton, whose SRA has admitted that it cannot make up its mind between the bidders, has sought to blame the government for 'dithering' over the issue!

The other regulators have not emerged looking much better. Her Majesty's Rail Inspectorate (a division of the Health and Safety Executive) has been criticised for an over-close relationship with the industry and has faced allegations that it has not been as vigorous in enforcing safety standards as its mandate requires. It is now fighting a lonely battle against the establishment of a new, dedicated rail safety regulatory authority, separate from the HSE.

As for Tom Winsor and his Office of the Rail Regulator, it was alleged that they were actually making the situation worse. Counsel for the Cullen Enquiry, Robert Owen QC, said that the ORR's pressure on Railtrack to improve performance could not be ruled out as a factor leading to conflict with railway safety.

Mr Owen, in his closing submission to the inquiry said that this tension may be partly due to, and reflected in, the economic regulatory regime, in particular on the mechanism for the imposition of penalties for poor performance in consequence of which fines of millions of pounds may be imposed by the regulator.

'The magnitude of penalties likely to be imposed for poor performance, and the gross disparity which exists between performance and safety sanctions, may convey the wrong message to the industry. Furthermore, that disparity may do little to dismiss any public perceptions which may exist to the effect that safety is being compromised in pursuit of performance.'

Mr Owen was actually echoing the Conservative Opposition claims that the regulator's role was a menace to safety, the only serious intervention into the crisis made by an official Opposition where decisions in government had done so much to contribute to the prevailing disarray. Shadow Transport Minister Bernard Jenkin asserted that Mr Winsor had 'failed to achieve the right balance between safety and performance . . . The Regulator is not sufficiently qualified to make judgements about safety, though this has not prevented him from making highly contentious statements about safety.'

The ORR's future in its present form is also in doubt. The House of Commons Transport Committee found that the regulation of Railtrack 'has also been . . . wanting, with serious weaknesses in the way in which the work expected from the company was specified, how its performance was monitored and how the company could be held to account.'

Mr Owen told the Cullen Enquiry that he saw merit in Alistair Morton's view that the regulator should be replaced by a board in order to make for a more de-personalised and less confrontational relationship with Railtrack. So the industry's regulators are all, to some degree or another, under a cloud. But none more so than the fourth – the ministers of the Department of Environment, Transport and the Regions, sitting at the apex of the entire structure.[19]

Here at this apex one found John Prescott, theoretically the second man of the government. Prescott should have been good news for the railways. The leading 'old labour' emblem of the Blair administration, he has had a record of support for public ownership and public service. His years as an active trade unionist in the merchant fleet, where workers are now represented by the mainly railway RMT union, should have stood the industry in good stead as well, despite the deputy premier's well-known fondness for his two Jaguars.

While Prescott's notoriously adversarial relationship with spoken English has led to an unflattering appraisal of his intelligence, this is unfair. It is rather his prickly nature, including an unwillingness to back down from proposals to which he has become personally committed, that has got in the way of his better judgement. This and the fact that the prime minister has determined all along to treat his deputy as a tiresome necessity rather than an asset. This dates back to Labour's days in opposition, when Blair held important meetings behind the deputy leader's back, even to the point of misleading him as to where and when they were taking place!

The extent to which Prescott lacked political influence where it counts was highlighted by his failure to persuade Downing Street to find room for his transport legislation (which, *inter alia*, put the SRA on a statutory footing) in the government's programme until three years into the parliament. Rather like his appointee at the head of the SRA, Sir Alistair Morton, Prescott was an audible and visible contributor to the general post-Hatfield crisis performance, without ever quite managing to come across as a contributor to the solution to the problems. He huffed at the TOC's fare increases, puffed at the SRA–Railtrack stand-off over the East Coast Main Line, harrumphed at the failures which left passengers stranded at Stansted Airport at midnight and was generally keen to be seen to be knocking heads together. Yet the longer and louder he huffed and puffed, the more obvious it became that the 'new railway' offered little scope for an interventionist-minded politician to intervene.

The situation was not of Prescott's making. Left to his own devices, there can be little doubt that he would have pressed ahead further and faster with remaking the industry which, just a few years earlier, he had openly favoured returning to public ownership. His agenda never seemed to find approval, however, with a government hierarchy which had one eye on the road lobby and the other on *The Daily Mail*. Influential Number Ten policy wonk Geoff Norris vetoed every proposal which he imagined might offend the road lobby in the government's first years. Tension between Prescott and Norris reached such a pitch that, in the end, transport had to be taken away from the latter's policy brief.[20]

Instead, Blair tried to curb his deputy's public transport and railway enthusiasms by lumbering him with a deputy as Transport Minister who marched to the beat of a very different drum. Lord Gus MacDonald was the fourth such deputy Prescott had had since 1997 and by some measure the most formidable. A former Trotskyist and activist in the Govan shipyard on the Clyde who later became a successful businessman and media baron in his native Scotland, MacDonald had two salient characteristics – a love of the private sector and a love of the great road economy. The likelihood of his spearheading the search for a solution to the crisis of the privatised railway industry was therefore, at best, remote. His Lordship did indeed unveil a major road-building programme while the rail disruption was at its height and was, at the same time, reported to oppose Prescott's desire to 'come down heavy' on the private rail companies (while being notably cool towards the railway unions).

Lord MacDonald is also cursed with a political tin ear, not an uncommon affliction among those politicians who never have to seek the endorsement of the electorate for their policies or opinions. So it was that he was unwise enough to deny to *The New Statesman*, in the course of an interview, that there was a railway crisis at all.

> I don't think it's getting worse and worse . . . Of the trains that should be running, 92 per cent are running, 50 per cent of the inter-cities are late and about 75 per cent are late by up to ten minutes on the London commuter lines. So, of 18,600 trains that should be running every day, there are about 500 that are more than half an hour late, so its about 3 per cent . . . it's a constant struggle to try and keep things in perspective.

As a display of ministerial indifference to the tribulations of everyday life, it could hardly be bettered. On MacDonald's logic, the country should be celebrating the fact that the great majority of the people who boarded the London to Leeds express which derailed at Hatfield eventually reached their destination.

MacDonald was immediately denounced by almost everyone with an interest in the subject, most tellingly by Liberal Democrat MP Don Foster who asked the minister to 'stop relying on silly surveys produced by Labour focus groups and start living in the real world that the rest of us inhabit.' *The Times* added that 'Britain cannot afford the complacency that Lord Macdonald's remarks suggest. The railways are in crisis, and the public is furious.'[21]

The danger for the government in Lord MacDonald's Marie-Antoinette impression was that it might, for the first time, make the public furious with *them*. Hitherto, exasperation with the state of the railways had been directed at other targets, with majority opinion holding, reasonably, to the view that this was a problem Labour had inherited rather than created. A survey conducted by MORI for *The Times* two months after Hatfield found that, when people were asked who they blamed for the disruption to transport in Britain, opinion divided as follows: Railtrack 45 per cent, the train companies 36 per cent, the previous Conservative government 33 per cent, the Labour government 24 per cent, with fuel protesters and global warming bringing up the rear in single digits.[22]

However, every passing month of unresolved disruption made it more likely that the incumbent government would start to carry the political can. The same survey revealed that young voters were twice as likely to blame the present government as the previous one for the transport turmoil.

Just a few months earlier, Prescott had been boasting of his ten-year transport plan. This promised £60 billion for the railways over the next decade, with the amount to be more or less evenly divided between public and private money. Using New Labour's staccato phrasing to the party's conference in Brighton, he claimed – incorrectly – that 'we'll see more invested in the next ten years than we saw in the last one hundred years. New track. New trains. New signalling. New services. New stations . . . In 2010 we will see 50 per cent more passengers on trains and 80 per cent more on rail freight.'[23]

Within a few weeks, this looked to be little better than fantasy. The reality was a 40 per cent drop in passenger numbers, a rise in road traffic of up to 25 per cent in parts of London, already the most congested city, and the certainty that more cars on the roads would mean more fatalities as well. Some analysts were speculating that it could be 2003 before numbers returned to pre-Hatfield levels. Railtrack itself reduced its projected passenger growth figure for the next ten years from 47 per cent to 37 per cent, although it blamed this on the government's increasingly car-friendly tax policies rather than the state of the railways.[24]

Even if passengers did in the end return to the railways, the post-Hatfield 'nervous breakdown' also made it clear that the industry was in no position to deliver on John Prescott's verb-free vision. Railtrack insiders were making it clear that it would be as much as the company could do to maintain the present network, never mind create all that 'New track. New trains. New signalling. New services. New stations.' The mere effort to keep the status quo more or less intact, when combined with post-Hatfield compensation claims and emergency expenses (running at around £580 million), seemed in danger of pushing the track monopoly towards bankruptcy. The company's debt burden is slated to rise to £8 billion by 2003. Interest payments on this would amount to £1 billion a year, so the banks would end up getting the public money earmarked for investment in the network.

The company approached the government for an advance on its ten-year plan money just to keep going. A first subsidy of £1.5 billion, announced in April, is unlikely to be the last. Railtrack managers remained deeply sceptical that, under these circumstances, anything like the private sector billions budgeted for under the ten-year plan could ever see the light of day. The company appears in fact to be walking away from any commitment to major improvement work.

SRA sources claimed that 'Railtrack is close to bankruptcy. It cannot survive as it is without the injection of further government money.' Railtrack denied this, but it has had to go along with Morton's recommendation that it should accept reduced responsibility for network improvements and major new projects, concentrating solely on the maintenance and operational end of its business. Amidst all this, its shares began to slide, making raising new money still more difficult.[25]

A *Financial Times* headline seemed to sum it up: 'Network disintegrates amid cycle of blame.' The accompanying article painted a 'picture of an industry spiralling in a seemingly unbreakable deadlock ... it is a cycle of blame that is hard to break because of the deteriorating relationship between many of the key figures', citing the differences between Prescott and MacDonald, Morton and MacDonald, Morton and Winsor, Morton and Railtrack, within the SRA and between Railtrack divisions![26]

So, with a near-bankrupt track operator enjoying a 'cancerous' relationship with its infrastructure contractors, frustrated and fragmented franchisees tottering towards insolvency amidst widespread opprobrium, a gaggle of squabbling regulators supervised by ineffective politicians, and public confidence at an historic low, what price the future of Britain's railways?

All research indicates that it will take some years before passenger confidence is restored in the system. Some business, both passenger and freight, may never come back. Long before Hatfield, a crisis of confidence had been developing in the privatised railway. The crash on the East Coast Main Line and the industry's response to the tragedy brought matters to a head. It was this response that pushed public tolerance with the privatised railway past breaking point. Compromised by 'fat cat' greed, undermined by years of inefficiency and unfulfilled promises, battered by accidents, the crisis of the winter of 2000–2001 finally forced the country to confront the legacy of privatisation.

It would seem reasonably clear that the damage done to the industry cannot be overcome within its present dysfunctional structure. If good can come out of disaster, it is that Hatfield has finally made that obvious. It has made inevitable some consideration of those alternatives which government and private business have hitherto chosen to ignore.

As the Railtrack poster displayed at every major station at the turn of the year put it: Sorry is not Enough.

6

Return Ticket To Public Ownership

Public service or shareholder value? The central question confronting Britain's rail industry under its present regime was summari-
sed in an exchange of opinions reported in April 2000, after the
Ladbroke Grove disaster and before Hatfield. Railtrack's then Chief
Executive, Gerald Corbett, delivered himself of a rather extraordinary
view: 'We have moved completely off the profit agenda and the
shareholder agenda. After we were privatised we stayed on a profit
and shareholder agenda for too long. We have now gone over to the
public service obligations agenda.'

The same newspaper report quoted the observations of a nameless
City analyst on Corbett's comments: 'The shareholders will kill him
if he comes out with this rubbish. His primary concern is to look
after the assets of his shareholders. We do not want any political
creeping for the sake of a knighthood. If he really believes that, it is
time he was put out to grass.'[1]

Six months later, Corbett was indeed out to grass (or on his way
to the boardroom of Woolworths, to be exact), with the knighthood
on hold. The shareholders-first philosophy did in fact dominate the

fag end of his leadership of Railtrack, right down to the dividend increase announced after the Hatfield crash. The only people killed were, of course, four of the unfortunate passengers on that train.

But the exchange highlights the central question facing the British people in considering what they want to do with their railways: is the industry a public service, or is it just another business? Should the needs of the shareholders (for profit) or those of the public (for a safe, reliable service) prevail?

The public seem to have made up their minds on the matter. They want a publicly run, public service, integrated railway. In this chapter we shall show why they are right and why the arguments of those clinging to the structure of the one hundred piece privatised railway are wrong.

Free-market dogmatists would, of course, deny that there is any requirement to make a choice between public service and private profit. In the arguments leading up to privatisation, enthusiasts for the 'new railway' asserted that by introducing the profit motive into the running of the industry, a far better service could be provided than under British Rail. There are good reasons for doubting that this was meant entirely seriously even by some of those who advanced the argument at the time. The Major government, in privatising the railways, based all its assumptions for the future on zero growth in the industry. The project was designed to offload an industry without a perceived future onto the private sector, on terms which would make it attractive to the City. It was a matter of giving sufficient incentive to private business to take on the task of managing decline.

The pro-privatisation lobby has been quick to claim credit for the growth in passenger and freight usage of the railway, surprising as it has been to them. It has been the only bright spot in an otherwise dismal picture. In Chapter Two, the flaws in this argument were explained. The improvement in the railway's prospects has had more to do with general economic growth, the increasingly apparent limitations of road transport and, in the case of freight in particular, artificially depressed demand in the last days of British Rail, than it has had to do with any initiative by the private companies.

On every other front – service, safety, network development – the record of privatisation has been deplorable. The drive for private profit – and a great deal of that has been squeezed out of the industry over the last seven years – has not delivered a safe and reliable service able to meet the needs of the community.

But even if a public-service railway is in conflict with a private-profit railway management system, does it fundamentally matter much whether the country chooses service before profit in this particular industry? Why not let the private companies do their best, or worst? That, more or less, appeared to be the attitude of Transport Minister Lord Macdonald when, in his notorious interview with *The New Statesman*, he dismissed concerns of a railway 'crisis'. The issue was not, he said, in the list of top ten political concerns as conveyed to him by Millbank's focus groups and, he said, only 7 per cent of journeys are made by rail.

The furore which greeted these remarks suggested he had mis-judged the public mood. More surprisingly, he had missed some fairly obvious points about transport. Take that 7 per cent of journeys – can the state of the roads be imagined if they were all undertaken by car rather than train, particularly in the rush-hour around London and other big cities, or on the motorways on Friday afternoons?

And would not the increased congestion represent an almost unbearable burden not only for those displaced from the malfunctioning railway but also for the 93 per cent already using the roads? Will people remain indifferent when the welcome flow of freight from road to rail over the last few years is reversed, and more and larger juggernauts clog up city streets and country lanes alike as a result?

MacDonald himself presumably thinks so. He compounded his original gaffe by, in April 2001, responding to a 10 per cent increase in fares announced by Virgin trains by urging people to use their cars instead. This position – a direct reversal of previous government policy – was an attempt to conceal ministers' unwillingness to do anything about Virgin's money-grabbing by passing the buck to individual travellers. The result of following the minister's advice would be increased congestion and more deaths on the roads (which in 1999 averaged more than nine per day in any case).

It is true that those who only use the railway occasionally – to return to see their family at Christmas, for example – may very understandably place the matter lower down their list of political priorities than the state of the local schools, or hospital waiting lists. But they are likely to be just as angry, and rightly so, when that Christmas is ruined because it is impossible to make the journey by train, as it was for so many at the end of 2000.

Of course, the railways in Britain are not likely, under any circumstances, to regain the place in national life which they held for around one hundred years, up until the 1950s. The development of the motor car is an irreversible fact of life, even if it has reached something close to its practical limits in environmental and economic terms in Britain today. The relatively short distance travelled for each journey, either passenger or goods, in a small country will always make the car, or road haulage, an attractive option, the more so given the billions of public money already invested in the roads network at very limited direct cost to the user.

But that does not make the railways either a luxury or an irrelevance. Governments of either party have, in words, recognised as much. The benefits of more people and more goods being carried by rail are uncontested. They are not expressed simply in individual terms – that it would be easier and more pleasant for a commuter to make the journey from the suburbs by train than by car, or that it could be commercially advantageous for the manufacturer to move more goods by freight train. The arguments are, at bottom, social: society will benefit as a whole, both economically and environmentally, if the car/road economy is only part of a public transport system which also includes, as its main complement, an extensive and efficient railway network. Just as it is presumed that society as a whole benefits from a well educated and healthy population, so too does it benefit from a modern railway.

The argument was put most passionately by Libby Purves, a columnist on *The Times*, in the midst of the chaos:

They just don't get it – not Corbett, not the present government, certainly not the smug survivors from the last disastrous bunch . . . what none of them grasps – even now, by the sound of it – is the utter centrality of the railway system to the maintenance of decent daily life in a crowded, complicated island. It is up there with the NHS and the police: an essential shared resource.

Purves went on to outline the human and commercial costs of the dysfunctional railway's post-Hatfield breakdown: the miserable lives of commuters, the strain on the Post Office, even the decline in attendance at West End theatres because people could not be sure of getting home afterwards. Her list could be extended considerably. Without decent public transport, normal life turned out to be impossible.[2]

This situation is unsustainable, even over the short to medium term. If people and companies cannot use the railway, they will make alternative arrangements, however hellish the roads may be. And, to accommodate them, the government will have to further bend public policy in favour of road-building and car use. The 'railway renaissance' will be over, the dismal no-growth assumptions of the Major government at the time of privatisation will have proved self-fulfilling and all the real and potential benefits of a sustained shift away from car and lorry use will have been squandered.

That is why the present debate on the future of the railways is so important. If something is not done to fix the railway network fast, then something else will happen instead – a major return to the roads. No one will stand up and argue that such a development would be desirable, but inertia could yet make it inevitable.

The starting point for the discussion should be the recognition of the public-service nature of the railways. They cannot be run simply as a commercial undertaking without regard to the wider social benefits that accrue to society from their efficient operation. That should apply to any company, of course, but the emphasis on private interests over public needs is particularly jarring in an essential service like the railways. That those social benefits cannot be accommodated within a private ownership framework is the clearest lesson of the last six years of the railway and the clearest indication that a return to public ownership is essential.

A few disagree. Firstly, there are those fundamentalists who still believe that, left alone, private industry will correct the problems and will yet deliver on its promises.

Keep it private

Let us quote Anthony Hilton, City Editor of *The Evening Standard*, as representative of what can fairly be called an extreme position under the circumstances. He wrote, post-Hatfield: 'Railtrack still functions as a company, so it can still get out of the mess. Laying track is not a difficult job – all it needs is a supply of rails, the money to pay for them, management to organise the project and time to do it. Left alone to implement its recovery plan . . . there is no reason why it shouldn't sort things out.' Laying track is, of course, not difficult. However, rail and management of required quality, and money in the required quantity are all things Railtrack lacks on a grand scale, and without them all the time in the world will not fix the railway.

Hilton also urged the rejection of any proposal to re-integrate track and train under the same, private, owners. 'A vertically integrated structure would mean that there could only be one operator per line. That would mean there was no competition . . . and no cap on fares. Cross-country services where the operator moves across rails owned by many different companies would also be a nightmare to negotiate.' As argued earlier, competition on the railways is 95 per cent chimerical and surely nothing could be more nightmarish than negotiating the commercial complexities of the present fragmented network. Hilton's solution? 'Give the Railtrack people, who got the railways into this mess, the room and resources to get out of it.'[3]

With an analysis so blind to the patent realities of the situation, it is not surprising that Hilton's conclusion is so implausible, and now finds almost no support anywhere. Railtrack has, of course, been given considerable public resources, with the promise of more to come. But even by its own admission it has lacked the ability to efficiently manage those resources, and the more 'room' Britain's biggest private monopoly has been given, the less the public interest has been served.

In similar vein, Rupert Darwall, a senior adviser to Norman Lamont when the latter was making his name as one of Britain's least successful Chancellors of the Exchequer, declared that 'competition is engine of change for railways'. He praised privatisation for having 'given managers much greater freedom to manage'. This argument is at least accurate, but we have all paid the price for that freedom. He advocates greater consolidation and integration of the industry within an exclusively private-sector framework.[4]

Urging 'evolution not revolution', Jim Steer, Managing Director of transport consultants Steer Davies Gleave praises the SRA for 'seeing no virtue in a command and control model'. He also credits Railtrack with having a more impressive strategy than British Rail ever managed (he must mean that it produces larger documents more frequently). Steer believes an 'industry accord', with Railtrack recast as a 'boring utility' (perhaps with a government stake) enjoying 'normal' profit margins is an adequate way forward.[5]

Richard Brown, Chief Executive of the trains division of National

Express (presently operating nine passenger franchises without great distinction), who is also the chair of the Association of Train Operating Companies, claims, perhaps unsurprisingly, that Hatfield was not caused 'by any fault in the structure of the industry as such'. He is therefore sceptical of the case for 'another round of major reforms'. But, again no surprise, he advocates a greater role for train operators in running track and network in their respective areas, without taking ownership away from Railtrack.[6]

It is obvious that none of these arguments fully addresses the problems generated by fragmentation, or by the need of all private parties in the industry, however reconfigured, to make a profit, often in competition with each other. And the day-to-day consequences of these problems are by now all too clear.

The most they hope for is that either a concentration of interests in fewer private hands or some measure of government regulation may make the difficulties disappear. They are not as extreme as Hilton's position – that it would be better if the government did less, changed nothing and left the private sector to get on with it. But they are all informed by a belief that private is best, unshaken by the evidence to the contrary in the story of the privatised railway. None of them addresses the apparent conflict between private operation and safety, a point to which even the head of Her Majesty's Rail Inspectorate has drawn attention.

In the wake of Hatfield, these arguments may seem overwhelmingly out of tune with both public opinion and practical reality. However, it should be borne in mind that possession is traditionally considered to be nine parts of the law, and that these arguments come from the people in possession (now that the laws have been made to enable this). These voices are representative of the considerable interests which have profited from the destruction of British Rail and the creation of the hundred piece railway, and wish to carry on doing so. It is a fact of life in Britain today, under 'new Labour' as under the Conservatives, that such interests are not easily dislodged, particularly when the political will seems to be lacking.

This leads to the second position which upholds the status quo – that of the government.

Labour's plan

'If it ain't broke, don't fix it,' runs popular wisdom. 'We admit it's broke, but fixing might make things worse' has less to commend itself as a plan. But that is the cornerstone of the government's approach to the railways. It is expressed in different ways: 'we have to take the world as we find it, not as we want it to be', 'we have to start from where we are,' and so on.

Behind what appear to be reasonable arguments lies a determination to assert that, whatever should be changed, it is not the fundamentals of the structure of the industry. This view has been given its clearest expression by Sir Alistair Morton, the man appointed by the government to oversee the railway. He took the opportunity of the publication of the Strategic Rail Authority's strategic 'agenda' – not, let it be noted, its strategic plan, which at the time of writing has still not made an appearance – to spell out his *laissez-faire* attitude.

In his preface to this document, Sir Alistair wrote:

The plan will not be a document laying down the SRA's instructions to the industry, designed to be obeyed in detail and

to govern every development and operation. Britain's rail system has been privatised and must respond to the demands of
users, to the market. Private sector capital and management
must produce those responses. The SRA will guide, facilitate,
encourage and support, taking the lead to resolve doubt,
develop consensus, accelerate progress, promote integration
and – with the Regulator and the safety regulator – insist on
standards. The SRA must guide and lead, but not command
and control.[7]

Sir Alistair's language follows closely that of Jim Steer, the transport consultant quoted above. While, however, the latter speaks only
for himself and his private clients, the former must be presumed to
be speaking for the government. So the Labour/SRA agenda is to
guide, but not command, build consensus but not control, accelerate
and promote but not, in the slightest way, to trespass on the newly
minted property rights of the private owners of the 'new railway'.

Given that private ownership has, to put it mildly, been so
problematic; given further that a return to public ownership would
be wildly popular with the public, and that Tony Blair's administration claims to set great store by such considerations; given that
just a few years ago such a move was the Labour Party's settled
policy; given all that, the first question to be addressed is why the
government's attitude to the industry is as it is. Only then can we get
to grips with what it is actually proposing by way of a substitute for
radical remedial action.

There are, of course, familiar practical arguments which ministers
are rehearsing against a return to public ownership. But the funda-

mentals of the government's hostility to a publicly owned railway have relatively little to do with the practical considerations.

There is, first, the desire to avoid acquiring ministerial responsibility for the state of the railways, a reluctance to be held to account for every accident and performance problem. This is an unworthy argument – why should politicians who aspire to run the country shrink from taking responsibility for public transport? It is also a futile one, since the public will ultimately hold government responsible in any case. If private industry fails, people may well first of all blame the private management. If, however, over a period of time the government of the day fails to address the underlying problem but allows those managers continued free rein in an important public service, then it is to the government that blame will increasingly attach.

Behind this argument lies a more profound one concerning the government's attitude to the industry and the economy as a whole. The railways are yet again being sacrificed on the altar of a particular ideological position – in this case New Labour's desire to appear 'business-friendly' and free of any taint of association with any 'old Labour' initiative, even one first undertaken by the 1945 government, the most celebrated in Labour's history.

In particular, the prime minister and the chancellor of the exchequer, whose views are decisive on this matter, worry about what sort of message would be sent to the world financial markets by the return of an industry or service to the public sector. It would call into question their commitment to the free market. Still more worryingly, it would signal that the many privatisations undertaken in Britain (and in other countries for that matter) over the last twenty years are not intrinsically irreversible.

This argument is consistent with the general thrust of government attitudes. The prime minister has made great play over a number of years of being uninterested in 'ideology' and only in 'what works and what doesn't'. Given that the privatised railway clearly has not worked and that pragmatism would in this instance require a speedy reversion to some form of public ownership, there must, in the end, be an ideology involved.

In fact, New Labour has, for all its claimed indifference to forms of ownership, actually pushed privatisation further on from where it was left by the Thatcher–Major years. The most notorious examples are the proposed privatisation of the management of the infrastructure of the London Underground and of the National Air Traffic Control Service. Under the guise of the 'Private Finance Initiative', privatisation has also been considerably extended in the health service, in education, in the management of prisons and even in the running of the armed forces.

In this sense, the debate about the future of the railways cannot be conducted in isolation from a much wider discussion about public versus private ownership, and about the prevailing view throughout the world that the former is invariably second best.

An examination of the whole issue is beyond our scope here, but the government's record is suggestive of two things. Firstly, the Blair government has an *a priori* preference for private ownership, private money and private enterprise over public service. The prime minister's occasional derogatory references to public sector workers (telling a business audience, for example, that he 'bore the scars' of his struggles with them) underline this.

Secondly, the determination to push on with the 'public-private partnership' on London Underground (again in the teeth of overwhelming public opposition) displays a singular unwillingness to draw conclusions from the failure of rail privatisation. Most of the disasters that have afflicted the railways are likely to be revisited on the London tube network under the government's plans – the separation of train operation from infrastructure maintenance (with the latter in private hands) above all.

So the government's actual plans for the railway need to be set against this background. Bad as the private sector may be, New Labour is not disposed to challenge it. Yet, so conspicuous are its failings in the railway sector that doing nothing is scarcely a credible position for any government. That was the case before the Hatfield crash, and it is still more the case after it. As a consequence, government strategy has been based on an attempt to do something without changing anything fundamental.

There have been two central pillars to this endeavour. First, there has been the establishment of the Strategic Rail Authority with the approach outlined by its first chairman above. Secondly, there is the ten-year plan for transport, with its promises of lavish public and private resources to modernise the railway, finally unveiled by John Prescott in the summer of 2000.

The SRA

In the previous chapter, the post-Hatfield record of the authority (then just emerging from 'shadow' status with its full statutory powers, such as they are) was scrutinised. It contributed little or nothing to the resolution of the prevailing crisis. It is impossible to evaluate the SRA's strategy because it has not yet been produced –

the plan is, in fact, running as late as a Virgin train in December 2000. It is not necessary to ask here whether the SRA is working, because the answer is all too obvious. But could it work, and play the part the government intends for it in the future?

There is no exact precedent for the SRA's role in the world of privatised industries. It has a remit which goes beyond that of those familiar shadows of the privatised monopolies, the regulators, with which the railway industry is in any case well supplied.

It is supposed, by cursing and cajoling, to herd the hundred piece railway into some coherent form and then nudge it forward in the direction indicated by the requirements of public service. For this, it has quantities of government cash for carrots, and the sanctions of the franchising and re-franchising process by way of sticks, although only for the train operating companies.

What it does not have is the control that can come from ownership alone. Derided for its lack of strategy and authority, the Strategic Rail Authority's greatest deficiency may be that it has no rail. At every turn it is confronted by the vested rights of private ownership. The meaning of those rights was vividly expressed by the anonymous City analyst in his condemnation of Gerald Corbett at the start of this chapter – shareholders first and don't you forget it, to paraphrase.

What shareholders want is a rising share price, increasing dividends and quick profits. If they don't see this in early prospect, they take their money elsewhere. The last point is particularly applicable in Britain's City-driven casino economy culture. As in the USA, but unlike Germany or Japan, City investors are notorious for their 'short-termism' – they want profits rapidly and a fast return on their investment. The length of time for which a shareholding taken in a publicly quoted company is held, on average, has been falling in Britain for over a generation. It is now just a matter of months. This volatility, and the unwillingness to commit to the long-term health and stability of an enterprise, is particularly inappropriate for an industry in which big investments like new lines or major upgrades of existing ones inevitably take many years to pay off.

The Channel Tunnel Rail Link has, for example, proved quite beyond the reach of the private financial markets alone, and government prodding and subventions have been required to get the thing built at all. The original Tory fantasy was that private enterprise would fund the link from scratch – the first new privately funded railway to be built in Britain for nearly 100 years. It never happened. Since the hole dug under Sir Alistair Morton's supervision opened, trains to Paris and Brussels have trundled placidly on slow lines through south London and the Kent countryside before stretching their legs on the high-speed line on the French side of the channel.

After a decade of procrastination and pass-the-parcel, the completion of the link has now been removed from Railtrack and handed over to Bechtel, the giant US construction company. But the taxpayer is paying for it, and it will still be many years before Eurostar trains are seen in London's St. Pancras terminal, projected end of the high-speed line. It will not be private enterprise that gets them there.

In this environment, the SRA must reconcile the interests of around one hundred different private corporations, each owing first loyalty to their investors, with the interests of the public. Few, if any, of these companies enjoy a good reputation with the public. Many stand as testimony to the truth that a pitifully incompetent management is not necessarily a barrier to making a tidy sum under the structure for the industry created by the last government. It is not a job for the faint-hearted.

The only strategic initiative to which the SRA is committed threatens to complicate things still further. This is, in effect, to split Railtrack's responsibilities in two. The existing company is to retain responsibility for maintenance and operations on the present network, perhaps under new ownership if it is taken over. Other businesses will be marshalled by the SRA to undertake major infrastructure projects, including any development of the network. These would surely include the big construction giants worldwide, like Bechtel, operating through a bewildering maze of joint ventures and special financial arrangements. Funding arrangements are to be negotiated on a project-by-project basis, but there is little doubt that the taxpayer will ultimately pick up most of the tab.

This would, no doubt, suit Railtrack pretty well. It could make its money out of access charges and property speculation, as at present, without having to worry about the financing and management of major projects, which seem to cause it problems out of all proportion to the return. The enhanced network would, in any case, end up back in Railtrack's portfolio under some terms or other once the work is done, unless the infrastructure itself is now to be under fragmented ownership. The arrangement might mean the more efficient completion of major railway engineering projects, although the record of the big construction companies is not all that government has cracked it up to be. Their involvement will certainly mean another set of private investors getting in on the act – looking for lucrative, low-risk returns at the taxpayers' expense – while increasing the industry's operational fragmentation.

Beyond that, the SRA's short-term plans for the future, outlined by Sir Alistair in the 'agenda' already quoted, indicate the authority's limited powers to actually get things done. He writes of 'completing consultation' on strategies, 'negotiating improvements where poss-ible', engaging in 'constructive detail with key stakeholders in the rail freight industry', developing 'funding and management structures', exploring 'the practicality of a number of ancillary development programmes', receiving 'the benefits of a number of completed multi-modal and rail-specific capacity studies' and, finally of 'completing the consultation process' – which is where he started. Then the plan is to be produced. It is not a programme to set the blood of the weary traveller coursing with enthusiasm. That is the job of the politicians.

Ten-year plan

Which leads us to the second leg of the government's strategy, the ten-year plan for transport unveiled by John Prescott in summer 2000. We have already seen that this plan has fallen victim to the over-selling rather typical of the government's approach to many issues, with exaggerated claims abounding.

John Prescott's £60 billion is made up of around £26 billion of taxpayers' money, with the rest coming from private sources. None of the latter is guaranteed. In the present state of the industry, there is scepticism about anything like that sum being found on the capital markets, and outright cynicism about the 'special funding vehicles' through which the government and SRA plan to raise it. These were described by one City analyst as 'the blind leading the blind'. He added that he could not envisage serious investors 'queuing up' to sink money in the risky railway.

Here the railway gets stuck in a catch-22 siding. The private companies can only raise the projected funds if the optimistic projections of growth in railway usage over the next ten years – 51 per cent in passengers and 80 per cent in freight – turn out to be credible. Only then can the necessary revenue be guaranteed to give investors the expected profitable return. Yet without the major improvements to the network projected as a result of this investment, the growth figures look less and less plausible. With confidence in the network deteriorating and no strategic leadership, private money will either go elsewhere, or demand a heavier guaranteed premium for investing in the railway.

The government could, of course, jump-start the process by putting its share of the stake up early. This might lead to visible improvements in service which might spread confidence around the sector. In fact, the opposite is happening. The government money is heavily 'back-loaded' – most of it is scheduled to appear in the latter part of the ten-year period. It is this that has had Railtrack pleading for subventions to be brought forward – not in order to embark on major investment projects, but merely to keep itself solvent and the existing network in some sort of repair, not to mention maintain dividend payments.

In April 2001 Railtrack was heading for debt levels which might require interest payments alone of over £1 billion a year before the ten-year plan is half completed. Clearly, this is not sustainable. Credit agencies are already warning that they may downgrade the company's debt, making borrowing still more expensive. And Sir Alistair

Morton was warning that the rising cost of merely maintaining the network was going to eat up the public funds available.[8]

The issue therefore is whether the government's ten-year plan for rail will do much more than keep the existing structure in being. Certainly, the government has no strategy for translating the considerable public subsidy flowing into the industry (and out of it into the pockets of shareholders in this remarkable public-private money-laundering racket) into a comparable level of control over it. This is despite the prodding of Labour MPs and even the willingness of Railtrack itself, at one point, to see the state take a stake by means of converting its subsidies into shares. Never has so much been given by so many to so few with so little in return.

This was underlined by the pitiful package of measures advanced by Prescott in April 2001, in pre-election recognition of the concern that the state of the railways was causing public opinion. In return for handing Railtrack £1.5 billion just to keep going ('not enough', the company complained as it promptly began lobbying for more), he secured the company's acquiescence in the appointment of a single 'public interest' director to the board. This individual would, however, share the same responsibilities to shareholders and the same requirements of confidentiality as other directors. Railtrack would, moreover, appoint this 'public interest' director itself!

As an additional sweetener, the company agreed that it would not make any exceptional or special dividend payments to shareholders for a five-year period. No restraint was, however, imposed on its ability to continue to raise its ordinary dividend by as much as it likes, a right the board has freely exercised.

On top of the original subsidy, ministers rushed forward with another large sum – just short of £500 million – to compensate Railtrack for a cut in the track access charges it can levy from freight operators, ordered by the rail regulator. Railtrack is therefore effectively indemnified by government against any negative financial consequences which might result from the regulator's public-interest decisions!

However, the mere hint of government intervention was enough to send the company's shares tumbling by more than 20 per cent. This makes it more difficult for the company to raise money on its own account, making the 'private' end of this public-private partnership still harder to envisage. The share price slump would at least make a return to the public sector cheaper to arrange. That may be the only way for Prescott to see any return for his money: no sooner had he announced this package than the train operators were clamouring for extra compensation to be paid them by Railtrack for the recent disruption. Little of this will be passed on to passengers.

It is therefore possible that the taxpayer will get no improvement in the railway at all for the £1.5 billion – the sum will be mostly swallowed up in inter-industry payments, compensation and, no doubt, large lawyers' bills. Still worse, another private company may be the beneficiary of the Treasury's largesse, according to reports that the government would rather see Railtrack sold to a construction giant outright than taken back into the public sector. This would represent the final capitulation of government to privatisation – subsidising a wholly owned subsidiary of a private monopoly. It would also, obviously, entrench rather than reverse the industry's fragmentation.

The SRA has missed the chance to play a useful role, if that was ever possible given its present powers and the structure of the industry as it is. Railtrack is a corporate basket case, with its 'public interest director' as much use under the circumstances as a sticking plaster on a broken leg. In a fragmented industry which has proved it cannot do even the simplest things efficiently, the government lacks any means for making its money work effectively, and in the public interest. With the one hundred piece railway, the government is pouring money into a well-holed bucket.

Certainly, that was the view of the House of Commons Transport Committee which, shortly before the general election, issued a report once again hauling Railtrack over the coals. The MPs declared it 'unacceptable that the taxpayer should be compelled to bail out a private monopoly company which has acted so incompetently, without taking any stake in the company in return.' The committee urged the government to either take a majority equity stake in Railtrack, or fully renationalise it. That, surely, is the fundamental question now facing the public and the industry.[9]

Public ownership

For twenty years or more, few people were prepared to trumpet the virtues of public ownership. To advocate the withdrawal of anything from the private sector was to be marked out as an anachronistic die-hard, or even an eccentric. Such argument as there was focused on whether, when and how industries and services should be privatised, never whether anything would be better done and run in the public sector once it was out in the privately owned jungle.

The great rail crisis has changed all that. When even *Daily Mail* columnist Lynda Lee-Potter, the strident voice of suburban middle

England, urges a return to public ownership, there is no doubt that the earth has moved. She observed that the railways were 'our assets and they've been sold off to exploiters who care more about profits and services', adding: 'Six years ago the Labour Party promised that when they came to power they would reverse privatisation. But they've reneged on that pledge.'

Lee-Potter is, on this issue, in company with the weight of public opinion. The most recent survey to hand reveals that a staggering 76 per cent of the population (including the great majority of Tory voters) want the railways renationalised. It is ironic that a government which generally follows closely the views expressed in Ms Lee-Potter's newspaper is on this occasion choosing to represent the minority 12 per cent who want the railways left under present management.[10]

When the possibility that this was the clearest of the many cases where public would be better than private – when letters first appeared in *The Times* asserting 'Never thought I'd say it, but I will. Come back BR, all is forgiven' – the government hurried to stamp the idea out.[11]

While ministers' motivation for dismissing the idea out of hand was no doubt rooted in the ideological predilections mentioned above, three arguments were advanced in the public arena. The first was that any change in structure or ownership 'would mean further upheaval and chaos' and the second was that 'it would cost too much' or, in a variation, that 'the money would be better spent on other things'. The third was that it would 'take too long'

The first argument really amounts to 'would public ownership mean a change for the better?', while the second asks 'is it practical given financial constraints?' The third is unworthy of detailed consideration – public ownership could certainly be introduced in less time than the three and a half years it took the government to set up the ineffectual Strategic Rail Authority.

The first argument is perhaps the more straightforward, and the one on which public opinion has most clearly made up its mind. The privatised railways have meant almost perpetual upheaval and chaos in an important public service. There is no sign that it can emerge from that chaos within its present framework. Attempts to patch up something workable from a mixture of private firms, sundry regulators and government cash seem more implausible with every week's news from the industry. No one with any understanding of the railways believes any longer that a private solution to the privatised disarray is possible (unless they are among those few personally profiting from the status quo).

Take a sampling of opinion from different sides. Mick Rix, General Secretary of the train drivers' union ASLEF, argued:

It is time that Railtrack was restored to the public sector. I do not offer this as a point of political dogma but as a practical and popular way of overcoming the industry's problems.

It would end the conflict between the shareholder interest and public interest. It would be a step towards rebuilding the stronger safety culture which was one of British Rail's better attributes. It would give the taxpayer a measure of control in return for the billions of pounds pumped into the privatised industry through subsidies. It would give the railways an accountable management, able to assist in the development of the government's integrated transport strategy. And it would make it clear that the buck stops with elected ministers, who would have the power and authority to direct this vital strategic industry.[12]

Jimmy Knapp, Rix's opposite number in RMT, the largest rail union, asked:

> ... why public ownership with regard to the railways and not with other privatised utilities? Because, whatever their failings, these utilities do not continue to receive the sustained levels of public subsidy that rail demands ... revenue support grants paid to the Train Operating Companies in 1999/2000 amounted to £1541.5 million, twice the level of support given to British Rail [in its last years].
>
> Experts suggest that as much as 25 per cent of this subsidy is absorbed in the costs of the privatised network, for example in transaction costs, profit margins, higher insurance (a whole new industry of 'railway insurance' has emerged since privatis-ation) and capital charges. Even the optimistic projections for subsidy reductions built into the franchise agreements did not envisage this support falling below £900 million per annum.[13]

This is not just the 'producer interest' speaking: support for the restoration of Railtrack, at the very least, to the public sector runs much wider. The former chair of the Save Our Railways pressure group, Jonathan Bray, says that this would be a force for stability: 'It would allow for integration of various policies and it would enable control of engineering functions at a senior level. It would also remove it from the "city casino" where shares rise and fall over perceived "impositions" of the rail regulator.'[14]

Oliver Raison-Shaw, who lost his father in the Ladbroke Grove crash, supported the launch of the trade union campaign to take Railtrack back into public ownership, saying that 'there cannot be safety on the railways in the present situation. Renationalisation is the only way to have a safe railway, with no conflict of interest from financial imperatives that outweigh safety. That is what has happened now with the fragmentation of the railways.'

The Labour chair of the House of Commons transport subcommittee, Gwyneth Dunwoody, an acknowledged authority on the industry, is forthright about the advantages of taking the track back into the public ownership. Confronting the 'upheaval' argument head on, she retorted

if there's not upheaval in the next five to ten years, there won't be an industry.

Unfortunately, the short history of privatisation has not convinced me of the efficacy of dividing the railway into myriad pieces when what we want is an integrated system.[15]

But would public ownership make enough of a difference? It would be foolish to argue that a change in ownership could immediately deliver an entirely safe, completely efficient railway. None of its advocates assert that. Britain's railways have, by most international standards, fallen too far behind. Nevertheless, if change is essential, and no durable improvements can be secured within the present structure, we must ask what change is needed and how can it be accomplished?

There are several different ideas. The New Labour think-thank, the Institute for Public Policy Research, has floated the idea of making

Railtrack a not-for-profit-trust. Tony Grayling of the IPPR advocated the trust option as

> a new form of public enterprise learning from the successful model that Canada has adopted for its air navigation services. This would be a true partnership with train operators, SRA, passengers and trade unions all represented on the board and none having a majority. A culture of co-operation and shared objectives would be institutionalised.[16]

There is much to commend this. However, more than a simple change of ownership of Railtrack is required if the industry is to work properly. Its relationship to other elements of the railway would also have to undergo a transformation. This has been addressed by the 'Take Back the Track' campaign run by the three rail unions, with growing public and political support.

The campaign urges that Railtrack be taken back into state ownership, as a public service. It has also demanded that the maintenance and repair work which the private monopoly has contracted out with such disastrous consequences be brought back in-house. Railtrack would itself manage the work, and directly employ the workers, ending the present conflict-by-contract.

All the railway unions remain committed, however, to restoring a publicly owned, integrated railway with returning Railtrack to the public sector as no more than the first step. It is the only coherent plan for putting the pieces back together again. The issue is how to get from here to there as quickly as possible.

If a publicly owned Railtrack was merged with the Strategic Rail Authority, there would be a real public-sector powerhouse at the heart of the network, able to steer development, enforce standards and run the infrastructure. That would then leave the train operating companies, freight operating companies and rolling stock leasing companies to consider.

The train operators are already, in many cases, near to being 'virtual companies'. They are 'brands', some as well known as Virgin, their logos painted on trains owned by a second party, maintained by a third and running on tracks owned by a fourth. In the short term, an SRA (already the franchising authority) in command of the network would be well placed to insist on higher standards of performance and on putting passengers first, on pain of the franchise being returned to the public sector. As franchises come up for renewal, this should be done in any case. Already one or two operators have talked about 'handing back the keys' for their franchise to the SRA, while others teeter on the edge of insolvency.

Far from being a setback, this would help the re-integration of the railways' management. While Railtrack may have become the officially designated villain in the railway pantomime, the train operators' failings should not be neglected. They have grown fat on public subsidy and in hardly any cases have offered any return for it in the shape of an improved service. As rapidly as necessary, the franchises should be taken back into the public sector. If the issue of compensation were to arise in any particular case, then the subsidies already received by the company concerned should be taken into account first. Over a relatively short period of time, a re-integrated passenger railway could be recreated by these means if that is the direction the government were to give the Strategic Rail Authority.

Integration and operational efficiency would also require restoring the main freight operations – EWS and Freightliner – to the public sector. This is the only way of securing the social objective of moving the transport of more goods onto the rails, and of striking a balance between the needs both of passengers and of freight in their use of a common network.

As train and track operations are re-integrated under public control, the need for the rolling stock leasing companies would start to evaporate. Their existence was predicated on the fact that owners of short-term franchises would be reluctant to make huge investments in buying trains which would long outlast the franchise in question – hence the expediency of leasing. The SRA could plan the industry's rolling stock requirements over a much longer term, and allocate and reallocate engines and carriages between different sectors as required. This should also help maintain and develop Britain's remaining train-building operations in Derby, Birmingham and York.

Such a phased reconstruction of a public service railway would, in fact, mean relatively little upheaval and could start to bring measurable benefits in a short period of time. In terms of the development of the railway – new lines, major upgrades, re-openings – the SRA would be in a much better position to implement its plans if it directly owned the network and (through its Railtrack operation) employed most of the people who work on it. The government, in funding such developments, would be in a position to indicate priorities without worrying about which might find favour with a private sector fixated on rapid returns.

But what about the private money anticipated under the ten-year plan? As indicated above, there is real doubt as to whether much of this money will actually see the light of day, and whether there will be many takers for the 'joint ventures' – really state-directed private–private partnerships – which are to be the vehicles for the investment.

The private sector will, in any case, only borrow this money, something the public sector could do for itself. A state railway could, moreover, do it less expensively, since lending to the public sector is a lower risk business. And it would not be besieged by shareholders demanding a quick payback.

Such a railway would be ultimately accountable to the public through the mechanisms of democracy, and by holding politicians to account for their stewardship of the industry. However, if additional security against abuse is required, it should be possible to retain the Office of the Rail Regulator in a revamped role, independently monitoring the performance of the new SRA against public interest criteria. The ORR could, as it does at present, set efficiency benchmarks for the industry, both in terms of service delivery and financial management, with the ability to make recommendations to parliament about public investment in the network. And it could order compensation for passengers in the event of unsatisfactory performance on particular routes.

Is it affordable?

Even some of those who allow that, yes, privatisation of the railways was a bad idea, and, yes, a return to public ownership might work better than the present system, still fall back on the argument that it's just too expensive.

At a purely practical level, this is a strange argument when Britain's finances are in such good order, with record budget surpluses and a massive £22 billion windfall in the treasure chest from the auctioning of mobile telephone licences. Strange, too, when the government is committed to putting around £26 billion of public money into the railways, and when large chunks of that money will end up enriching private shareholders rather than building a better railway.

Given the benefits which would flow over the long term from a return to a public-service railway, it could easily be argued that even if taking Railtrack back into the public sector were actually to cost the less than £3 billion its May 2001 stock market valuation would require, it would be money well spent. But there are, of course, other methods of financing this kind of transaction, methods such as those used by the Attlee government – and many since – to take a great deal more than the railways into public ownership at times of much more straitened public finances.

The simplest way to take any company into state ownership is to issue government bonds to shareholders. This was the method used in 1947. These would be exchanged for shares, and the interest on them could be met out of the profits of the reinvigorated rail industry, spread over a number of years. Under this self-financing form of public ownership there would be next to no cost up front for the government, and no diversion of resources from the NHS or any-where else. As it happens, there is a great appetite in the City for more Treasury bonds at the moment, since they offer a stable and guaranteed income to complement more volatile stocks in the port-folio. There would therefore be no difficulty in placing bonds – basically claims on government debt – on the market.

There is also a perfectly valid argument for discounting the subsidies paid by the taxpayer to Railtrack from the purchase price. These are currently around £1.3 billion a year. This government money has been used, *inter alia*, to prop up Railtrack's shares, which remain at a higher level than might be expected because shareholders are certain that government subsidy will ensure future profits. Were the government to announce an end to subsidy tomorrow, the value of Railtrack would all but disappear. Under the procedure for restoring a public railway suggested in this chapter, there would be no need to compensate anyone else – franchises could be taken back, trains simply bought by the railway from the banks which own them and maintenance work re-integrated.

The simple bond-issuing procedure, of which ministers affect to know nothing, has long been advocated as a possible solution to the problem of the rail industry. As far back as 1995, when Labour was still committed in principle to renationalisation, *The Times* pointed out:

> . . . the Treasury could easily 'afford' to buy back Railtrack. Renationalisation would simply require an exchange of one kind of financial paper – government bonds – for another – Railtrack shares. This exchange would increase the public sector borrowing requirement for only one year . . .
>
> The value of Railtrack shares would depend directly on the rate of return to investors permitted by government regulation. If Labour chose to alter the regulatory framework and sharply reduce the prices charged by Railtrack, the company would immediately become much cheaper to buy back.[17]

Tony Grayling, the advocate of the not-for-profit trust, proposes the same course: 'The cost to taxpayers of buying out Railtrack's shareholders need not be great. The money could be raised by issuing government guaranteed private sector bonds, a facility provided for the Channel Tunnel rail link. In effect, Railtrack's profits would be converted into interest payments.' *The Times'* Anatole Kaletsky has written that buying Railtrack shares would be 'a fiscally sound alternative to repaying the national debt,' and more prudent than the chancellor's policy of fuel tax cuts for road hauliers.[18]

Jimmy Knapp of the RMT argues for the same approach, urging the government to issue

> . . . interest-bearing bonds for the shares of the company. This would give the government, or SRA if it was the agency chosen to run the company, immediate and direct control of its operations. The basis of compensation for the holders of shares would be the stock market valuation at the time of sale, or other specified date. Bonds would be issued bearing a fixed rate of interest, specified at that time, applicable over a period of years to be determined.[19]

So the fiscal argument against public ownership holds up no better than what one might call the 'chaos theory' deployed in support of the status quo.

It remains, then, to consider one final argument – that public ownership might lead back to the worst aspects of the old British Rail. Understandably, there is now a widespread view that, even at its worst, British Rail was still a far better run railway than the present mess. Nevertheless, nostalgia should not blind us to the necessity of a better form of public service railway than the traditional model fashioned by the 1945–51 Labour government.

A new public ownership

The process of renationalisation described above would address the problems which arise from fragmentation. The one hundred piece railway would rapidly become whole again. That is the first prerequisite for addressing the railway crisis. By removing the private profit element, it would also allow safety and service to become top priorities once more. Accidents would still happen, but they would never again be due to negligence or mismanagement arising from a desire to protect the shareholder interest above all. A re-integrated workforce and management would, in itself, be vital to re-establishing the safety culture which was once the railways' pride.

But more is required. British Rail had two stubborn flaws which a renewed public railway would not wish to reproduce. The first, located within the corporation itself, was a perceived disregard for passenger interests (although this may have been exaggerated). The second, to do with the form of public ownership, was that its plans and development were forever at the mercy of a penny-pinching Treasury.

In the first respect, there is something to be gained from the experience of the SRA, on which the passenger interest is represented. Regional and national passenger councils have also accumulated considerable experience, and could be a supplementary democratic voice in the running of the railway, pinpointing problems and promoting improvements. A return to public ownership must be accompanied by a real move towards 'passenger power' if it is to realise its potential. At present, passenger representative groups, for all the good work they do, can often seem like just another part of the maze of bureaucratic railway organisations. It will be a challenge to engage the regular train user in the work of thinking about the future of the railway, but if passengers can become convinced that their views will actually be listened to and acted upon by publicly accountable managers, it should surely be possible.

Likewise, there should be an institutional voice for the industry's long-suffering workforce, still the repository of most of the experience on how to actually keep things moving.

Local authorities too, should have a greater part to play in setting service requirements for their own area within an overall national network plan. If the government pursues its proposal to establish regional assemblies throughout England, these would be an appropriate level of local government to take a really constructive part in planning and developing the network. By extending the principle already embodied in the Passenger Transport Executives which already exist in many parts of the country, such regional bodies could ultimately exercise a guiding role over train services covering all but inter-city routes.

And why not give more of a say to those (again including local authorities) who wish to see more goods moved by rail? Both the environment and industry would benefit from a much greater priority for rail freight.

Other improvements for the passenger could easily be introduced. A return to simplified ticket pricing would be widely welcomed. The present bizarre and baffling range of options – APEX, saver, super-saver, open return, business return, some available on some trains on some days (but not unless you book in time), others on other trains until the ticket you want is sold out on the particular train you want

– should be scrapped. It leaves very few convinced that they are getting a good deal and very many confused, owing everything to mathematical models of revenue maximisation, and nothing to customer service. A simplified replacement based on route mileage, with clear discounts for off-peak travel, should suffice.

No one wants a return to the British Rail sandwich of yore, but neither is anyone satisfied with the over-priced processed food on offer to standard class passengers at present (first-class travellers do much better on Virgin Trains – they are the only ones allowed to dine on the country's main inter-city route). French railways, for example, subcontract the running of the catering to a restaurateur – an example of private–public partnership which could be emulated.

That is not all that could be learned from abroad. Swiss railways stable spare trains, with a driver, in sidings at regular intervals ready to take over if a locomotive fails on a service. How much time could be saved on Britain's railways through the adoption of such a practice? Why not match the Swiss guarantee of 95 per cent of trains arriving within four minutes of the scheduled time? (Britain's network struggles to deliver 90 per cent within ten minutes even when there's no particular crisis.) Or even the Japanese record of 99 per cent of trains on time!

There are other simple improvements to be considered. Liberated from the religion of reducing the head-count, perhaps all stations could once more be staffed for the whole time they are open (there are 200 unstaffed stations in the area covered by the First North Western franchise alone, for example). This would encourage more rail travel, particularly amongst women and late at night, when travellers feel more vulnerable.

Stations themselves could be rebuilt and re-designed over time. Too many outside the major centres resemble little more than bus shelters, invoking neither comfort nor pride.

A public railway could also plan its land-use, ending the pointless sell-off of property which cripples the railway's prospects for growth, particularly in the freight sector. While turning railway land into a station car park may encourage rail use, turning it into a supermarket has no such beneficial spin-off.

And why should the railways of France be so far in advance in terms of high-speed trains? Why should Japan be developing magnetic bullet-trains, while Britain's industry struggles to clear leaves from the line?[20]

Not all of this may be possible straightaway. But none of it is fantasy. Britain can have a railway worthy of the country which invented the system. The only fantasy was the Major–MacGregor one – the idea that the privatised industry could ever get us there.

Such a new public railway would be ultimately accountable to parliament through ministers, as is the National Health Service, for example. Its priorities could be debated and decided in the light of resources available each year, and over a longer period when it comes to planning major projects.

How should this railway be funded? In the end, investment in the railways should reflect the priority society places on sustaining a decent network, rather than the hope of turning a quick profit. That priority has surely risen as Britain looked into the abyss, since October 2000, of a country without a properly run railway. If the railways are indeed a public service, then a large element of its funding will and should be public in origin.

But that is not to say that the public railway of the future should be tied, on a month-by-month basis, to the apron-strings of the Treasury. The government has conceded the point in principle, by setting out a ten-year funding and modernisation programme, even if it is one that the present industry cannot deliver. If more is required in future, there is no good reason why a publicly run railway should not have the right and the ability to borrow money on the capital markets in the same way that private companies do, perhaps subject to the supervision of the rail regulator. The government has already conceded this right to two public bodies – the Post Office (rebranded Consignia) and Manchester Airport.

Only Treasury dogma about accounting for any debts held by public bodies (a dogma Gordon Brown has turned into a phobia) precludes such a sensible course of action. Naturally, resources would not be limitless, but a well run railway enjoying higher passenger and freight usage should have no great difficulty in raising cheaper additional funds for investment at rates which could well be met from the surplus generated by a better run, expanding, railway.

Whether investment is sourced from borrowing in this way, or directly from the taxpayer, it needs to be sustained over a number of years as part of an integrated public transport strategy. That investment is being proposed by the Labour government. Under privatisation the money is pouring into a system geared towards self-enrichment for shareholders and incapable of giving any value to the taxpayers for their money.

Public money must be matched by the public direction that can only come from public ownership. This has been the cornerstone of those railways elsewhere in Europe and the world which now excite the envy of visitors from Britain. Foreign railways, from Japan to France and even to India, may vary in their structure and operational management, but all deliver a better service to the public than does the network in Britain, because all are regarded as public services to be publicly funded.

Privatisation has been a tragedy for Britain's railways. That lesson has been learnt in blood, sweat and tears over the last six years, and experts flock here from all over the world to learn how to avoid repeating the tragedy in their own countries – even the pro-free-market European Union is using it as a case study on how not to run a railway.

All the evidence is that politicians who grasp the nettle of renationalising the railway will lose nothing in terms of public esteem or votes. Banishing the one hundred piece railway to the past will earn some political leader a place in the history books.

There is a still larger lesson to be learned from the whole privatisation experiment, and this is the lesson that the rigours of the market and the profit motive are not the only, or even the best, guarantors of progress and development, and that society needs to base its choices on different criteria altogether. Of these criteria, public service is the most important. If the experience of Britain's railways marks the end of the line for the disastrous political supremacy of privatisation and the free market, and raises society's vision once more to the alternatives to capitalism, then all the suffering described here will not have been in vain.

Notes

Foreword

1. I do not purport to do justice to the position or the evidence of any of those who gave evidence or whose views were reported, nor of the many bodies whose actions were considered. Nothing herein should be considered as authoritative in any way. These are very much personal observations, partial and prejudiced.

2. One is reminded of the words of Chief Justice Lord Denman over 150 years ago in relation to train operators: 'The supposition ... of free competition of carriers on the same railway is practically little else than absurd ... the very nature of the mode of conveyance forbids a free competition of rival carriers.' *R v London and South Western Railway* (1842) 1 QB 558 at 587.

3. Adrian Vaughan, *Railwaymen, Politics and Money*, London: John Murray, 1997, pp. 209–12.

4. Neatly précised in *British Railway Disasters*, 1996, Ian Allan Publishing, pp. 179–82. The disaster killed eighty people of whom twenty-two were children on a Sunday School outing.

5. Paragraph 46 of the Clapham Report, cmd. 820, 1989.

6. Lord Cullen's report is shortly to be published.

1   Trains and Money

1. *The Sunday Times*, London, August 29 1993.
2. Jack Simmons and Gordon Biddle (eds), *The Oxford Companion to Railway History*, Oxford: OUP, 1997, p. 228.
3. ibid., p158.
4. Paul Salveson, *British Rail: The Radical Alternative to Privatisation*, Manchester: CLES, 1989, p. 55.
5. *ibid.*, pp. 76–77.
6. Roger Freeman and Jon Shaw (eds), *All Change: British Railway Privatisation*, Maidenhead: McGraw-Hill, 2000, p. 22.
7. *A History of the LNER, Vol. 3: The Last Years, 1939–48*, by Michael R. Bonavia, London: George Allen & Unwin, 1983; European Community Directive 91/440, published by CAEF, Liverpool.
8. *The Financial Times*, January 17 1995.
9. *The Evening Standard*, November 30 1992; *The Independent on Sunday*, January 24 1993.
10. British Rail management information brief, April 28 1993; also available in *House of Commons Transport Committee*, London: HMSO, 1993.
11. *Private Eye*, October 1999.
12. *Rail Bulletin*, October/November 1995.
13. Freeman and Shaw, p. 19.
14. Paper presented to TSSA EC meeting, November 4/5 1993.
15. BBC Radio 4, December 20 1992.
16. Quoted in 'Down the Tracks of Change' by Barry Howe, *Global Transport*, Spring 1995, p. 52; *Jane's World Railways*, August 1992.
17. *The Daily Telegraph*, October 13 1995.
18. Philip S. Bagwell, *The Transport Crisis in Britain*, Nottingham: Spokesman, 1996, p. 153.
19. *The Independent*, January 23 1993.

2   The One Hundred Piece Railway

1. Hugh Montefiore, in *The Daily Telegraph*, January 5 1993.
2. *Rail*, January 24 2001.
3. *ibid.*
4. *Railway Gazette*, March 15 2001.
5. *Private Eye*, October 1999.
6. *The Independent on Sunday*, November 26 2000.
7. All company figures are the most recent as of March 2001, taken from their respective corporate websites.
8. Roger Freeman and Jon Shaw (eds), *All Change: British Railway Privatisation*, Maidenhead: McGraw-Hill, 2000, p. 109.
9. *Railway Privatisation: Passenger Rolling Stock*, Department of Transport, January 1993, p. 19; *The Observer*, October 10 1999.
10. *Rail*, November 15–28 2000.
11. *ibid.*
12. Freeman and Shaw, p. 74.
13. All statistics from the *Bulletin of Rail Statistics*, Quarter 1, 2000/01.
14. Freeman and Shaw, pp. 179–80.
15. *Railtrack 2000 Network Management Statement for Great Britain*, London: Railtrack, pp. 77, 83.
16. *OAG Rail Guide*, June 2001, page 7.

3   The Three Hundred Piece Railway

1. *Report on Seminar – Employee Perspectives on Railway Safety*, published by the Cullen Enquiry.
2. *Report prepared by Ex-BR Managers*, June 1993.
3. *The Daily Telegraph*, October 13 1995.
4. *The Sunday Telegraph*, February 25 1996.

5. *The Sunday Mirror*, April 1 2001; *Report prepared . . . p. 6.

6. Roger Freeman and Jon Shaw (eds), *All change: British Railway Privisation*, Maidenhead: McGraw-Hill, 2000, p. 68.

7. BBC News Online, April 17 2000.

8. Transcript of proceedings (day 19) of Southall and Ladbroke Grove Joint Inquiry into Train Protection Systems, p. 3ff.

9. *The Guardian*, December 19 2000.

10. *The Financial Times*, April 30 1996.

11. Keith Harper, 'Railway safety sold down the profit line', *The Guardian*, March 14 1998.

12. *The Safety and Health Practitioner*, October 1993.

13. *The Times*, August 17 2000.

14. *Railtrack's Network Stewardship*, TSSA summary, June 30 1999.

15. *The Financial Times*, May 7 2001, February 22 2001.

4 Sweat and Tears on the Tracks

1. Jack Simmons and Gordon Biddle (eds), *The Oxford Companion to Railway History*, Oxford: OUP, 1997, p. 533.

2. Adrian Vaughan, *Railwaymen, Politics and Money*, London: John Murray, 1997, pp. 316–17.

3. Simmons & Biddle, *op.cit.*, p. 482.

4. *TSSA Journal*, February/March 2001.

5. *The Financial Times*, January 4 2001.

5 Sorry Is Not Enough

1. *Keeping Track Bulletin*, December 2000; *Rail Professional*, January 2001.

2. *Modern Railways*, January 2001.

3. *Rail Professional*, December 2000; *Rail*, November 29 2000.

4. Ananova, January 3 2001.

5. BBC News Online, December 6 2000.

6. *Modern Railways*, December 2000.

7. *The Guardian*, December 28 2000; *Rail*, January 24 2001; *The Independent*, January 8 2001.

8. *The Financial Times*, January 8 2001.

9. *The Times*, November 29 2000; *Railway Gazette*, January 18 2001.

10. *The Observer*, November 12 2000.

11. *The Guardian*, November 29 2000; *The Guardian*, December 11 2000; *The Daily Telegraph*, February 14 2001; *Keeping Track Bulletin*, December 2000.

12. *The Financial Times* January 29 2001; *The Financial Times* November 27 2000.

13. *The Observer* November 12 2000.

14. *Modern Railways*, January 2001; *Keeping Track Bulletin*, December 2000; *Rail*, January 10 2001.

15. FT.com, January 10 2001.

16. *The Observer*, November 19 2000; *The Independent on Sunday*, December 3 2000.

17. *The Guardian*, January 2 2001.

18. *The Times*, February 26 2001.

19. *Rail*, November 15 2000, January 10 2001.

20. Andrew Rawnsley, *Servants of the People*, London: Hamish Hamilton, 2000, p. 297.

21. *The Evening Standard*, December 7 2000; *The Times*, December 8 2000.

22. *The Times*, December 19 2000.

23. John Prescott, text of speech to Labour Party Conference, Brighton, September 25 2000.

24. *The Guardian*, December 30 2000.

25. *The Guardian*, February 19 2001; BBC News Online, February 19 2001.

26. *The Financial Times*, May 4 2001.

6   Return Ticket To Public Ownership

1. *The Observer*, April 2 2000.
2. *The Times*, November 21 2000.
3. *The Evening Standard*, November 24 2000.
4. *The Daily Telegraph*, December 4 2000.
5. *The Railways: Where Do We Go From Here?*, Transport 2000, London, March 2001, pp. 11–13.
6. *ibid.* pp 23–7.
7. *Strategic Agenda*, published by the Strategic Rail Authority, March 2001, p. 1.
8. *The Observer*, April 22 2001; The *Guardian*, February 24 2001; *The Financial Times*, February 22 2001.
9. *Rail Investment: Renewal, Maintenance and Development of the National Rail Network*, sixth report of the Environment, Transport and Regional Affairs Committee of the House of Commons; BBC News Online, March 29 2002.
10. Quoted by Roy Hattersley in *The Guardian*, November 27 2000.
11. *The Times*, November 26 2000.
12. *The Guardian*, November 14 2000.
13. Transport 2000, *op.cit.*, p. 15.
14. *The Guardian*, December 19 2000.
15. *The Financial Times*, February 14 2001.
16. *The Guardian*, January 10 2001.
17. *The Times*, January 16 1995.
18. *The Guardian*, January 10 2001; *The Times*, November 30 2000.
19. Transport 2000, *op.cit.*, p. 16.
20. *The Times*, April 17 2001; *The Financial Times*, October 14/15 2000.

Postscript

The state of Britain's railways was not much of an issue during the General Election of June 2001. It's not that nobody cares – more that a conspiracy of silence suited an opposition which had created the present catastrophe and a government which had done nothing to remedy it. Yet it has been an issue ever since.

In the months since this text was completed, Lord Cullen has found that Railtrack was responsible above all others for the dreadful Ladbroke Grove crash, and has also criticised the shortcomings of Thames Trains and the negligence of Her Majesty's Rail Inspectorate.

Railtrack itself has shown its contempt for the public by asking for, and getting, an extra £1.5 billion government subsidy just to keep going, and then passing a full 10 per cent of this total on to its shareholders in a dividend payment on the very same day. Railtrack also announced – in the very week that Lord Cullen published his report – a handsome £1.5 million pay-off for Gerald Corbett, the failed chief executive in charge at the time of the Ladbroke Grove crash. Railtrack's share price has crashed throught the floor – as has the number of trains arriving on time, according to the latest figures.

Elsewhere, John Prescott and Lord MacDonald had their disastrous stewardship of the transport portfolio terminated in the post-election reshuffle, with Stephen Byers taking over. The latter's only rail-related initiative to date has been to plod on doggedly with the plans to part-privatise London Underground, threatening to create a Railtrack beneath the capital. Most recently, the government has tried, and failed, to silence its most trenchant parliamentary critic on transport matters, Gwynneth Dunwoody, by removing her from the relevant select committee. Sir Alistair Morton has announced that he is to step down as head of the Strategic Rail Authority, squabbling to the last with all and sundry over who should bear the blame for the great rail fiasco. And there is a growing cacophony of expert voices proclaiming that the government's ten-year plan for the industry is as good as dead.

At every turn, however, the government rules out any return to public ownership. Yet every development in the industry since Labour's re-election is confounding that position and, I believe, confirming the argument set out here that there really is no serious alternative.

Andrew Murray
London, July 2001

Index